CW00869152

Winning in Life and Work
Volume 1

Winning in Life and Work Volume 1

Compiled by Keith Blakemore-Noble.

Contributors: Keith Blakemore-Noble, Graham Phoenix, Cindi Wilson, Ruth Thirtle, Kim Davey, Ian Douglas, Claudia Crawley, John Brant, Patricia Duffy, Vincent Delaney, and Gary Setterfield.

Foreword by Johnnie Cass.

Hardback ISBN: 978-1-291-09676-7

Paperback ISBN: 978-1-291-09677-4

Disclaimer

Every care has been taken to make the figures and specifics in this book as accurate and relevant as possible at the time of writing. However, it is hoped that you will understand that these can change dependent on market and economic forces beyond the authors' control. The content, projections, figures, and indications contained in this book are based on opinion and cannot be relied upon when making investment decisions. The authors offer this information as a guide only, and it should not be considered as financial advice in any way. Please refer to your independent financial advisor who is qualified to give you complete advice based on your circumstances.

The advice and strategies contained herein may not be suitable for your particular situation, and you should consult with a professional where appropriate. The authors are not qualified to give financial, medical, or health advice. Please seek legal and financial advice from a qualified advisor before making commitments. The authors accept no liability for decisions made based on the content of this book.

While the publisher and authors have made their best efforts in preparing this book, they make no warranty or representation with respect to the accuracy or completeness of the contents of this book, and specifically disclaim any implied warranties of merchantability or fitness for a particular purpose. No warranty may be created or extended by sales representatives nor by written sales materials. Neither the publisher nor authors shall be liable for any loss of profit or any other commercial damages, including but not limited to special, incidental, consequential, or other damages.

Table of Contents

Foreword

by Johnnie Cass - International Speaker, Coach, Author and Trainer.

Whether it be addressing large audiences or working one to one, it has always been my great pleasure to work with many talented and gifted people across the globe. Over the last 10 years I have had the privilege of working with thousands of individuals to design and live a life that they love. It is always an honour to see the delegates that come through my programs step out into the new and the unknown. Many people talk about having the courage to try new things and move beyond their comfort zones but few actually do.

I was fortunate enough to be present when these aspiring thought leaders and experts decided to create this compilation book for your enjoyment.

Each of them is a thought leader in their respective field who has contributed to this diverse and wonderful book full of wisdom and great insights.

There is no doubt that life sometimes doesn't quite go the way that we planned. Whether it is challenges in our personal lives, our career or even sometimes we simply feel like we need to get our 'headspace' or 'heart space' back on track then this book offers something for everyone.

Each of the contributors shares with you their stories and insights as well as lessons learnt along the way on this great journey that we all share together called life. Through their unique expertise, their hope is that you may gain from their vast depths of knowledge and lessons on their chosen subject.

Although the subjects may be diverse I feel that there is something in this book for everyone. Whether you want to improve your levels of confidence, or perhaps you would like to gain a deeper connection in your intimate relationship, or possibly you may want to nail that job interview? Each chapter gives you solid take home tips and advice to help you at winning in life and work.

As I read through each of the contributors' expertise, I found that each of them had their own style and every story or topic covered proved to be very insightful. Some of their stories will move you and others will bring a smile to your face. Whether you choose to read one of the chapters or the entire book is entirely up to you as the reader. However I feel there is something wonderful to be learnt on all the pages written within this book. In fact you may find that by reading the stories from a totally unrelated topic to whatever problems you are experiencing in your life right now you may be pleasantly surprised as to how another contributor's expertise helps you in an unexpected way.

Each of the experts draws on their own levels of experience and one of the things I most enjoyed about reading this book was that even though they are clearly knowledgeable on their topics, their ability to keep things uncomplicated and straightforward will be much appreciated.

I am more than confident that within the pages of Winning in Life and Work you will have many light bulb moments and most certainly some clear strategies as well as wisdom from some prominent thought leaders and well versed experts.

Be Well and Be Amazing

Johnnie Cass

Introduction

We are all seeking to do the best we can in this game called life, aren't we?

But sometimes, no matter how hard you try, you just can't seem to find the key, that little nugget, which helps you to step up your game and win. You know that it is possible to win as you see many others around you doing so every day, but there are times when we could do with a little helping hand, some guidance to point us in the right direction.

That is what this book seeks to provide. Treat it as your secret weapon (although not so secret that you won't want to tell family and friends about it, so that they too can start to win more powerfully!) in the game of life. Read it carefully and often, for you never know when the right nugget will reveal itself at precisely the right time for you.

This volume contains the distilled wisdom from eleven international current experts in their respective fields, including confidence, relationships, interview techniques, property, grief management, overcoming chronic illness, and more; each of these experts have created a chapter specially for you, covering many key aspects and areas of life, both in your personal and professional life.

I cannot emphasise enough the value to you of reading and rereading all of these chapters, even if they may not at first appear to be directly relevant to you; for each chapter operates at multiple levels, and while a given chapter may at first appear only to be relevant to a specific personal or business aspect of life, careful reading, rereading, and meditation on it may reap many benefits in other areas of your life. There is one chapter in particular, which at first glance appears to be focusing on a very specific topic, but whose content and underlying message is almost certain to be of relevance across whole sections of your life. And no, I'm not going to tell you which chapter it is, for that you will have to discover for yourself (and what a discovery awaits you!).

However, as the old proverb rightly puts it, "You can lead a horse to water but you can't make it drink." Alas simply owning or holding this book is not going to help you to make any long-term changes. Not even just reading the book is going to result in major changes to your life. You must also take action as a result of what you have read; for it is only by taking action that we begin to make the changes that we seek in our lives, and by continuing to take action that we guide our lives in the wondrous directions we choose for ourselves.

On behalf of all of the contributors, may I express the hope that you enjoy this book, read it, act upon it, treasure it, and refer to it often. And may doing so reward you in ways you have yet to even consider imagining!

Keith Blakemore-Noble,
October 2012.

Conquering Shyness and Creating Self-Confidence

by Keith Blakemore-Noble

Keith Blakemore-Noble, The Confidence Alchemist™, is a speaker, author, coach, actor, trainer, and mind changer. Through the use of his unique Ultimate Confidence system (which he has carefully developed and refined and continues to enhance as brain and behavioural sciences evolve), he helps people to conquer their shyness and to unmask their confidence. This helps them to find their voice (be it for speaking from stage, speaking in team meetings, or just having the confidence to raise their hand and ask questions in seminars), and ensures that his clients are in a far better place to be able to connect with other people in social and business situations, resulting in them leading happier and more fulfilling lives – and who doesn't want that?

A living embodiment of the cutting-edge sciences and tools he employs, he has used them all on himself first, so he knows how well they work and also understands how the processes feel from your perspective.

Prior to moving full-time into helping people, he spent thirteen very successful years in IT (where as a Chartered IT Professional he attained the highest level of Fellowship of the BCS, IT's chartered professional body) including leading a team with members in the UK, Norway and New Zealand; this means he has gone from reprogramming and upgrading computers, to reprogramming and upgrading people's minds! The latter is infinitely more rewarding, it has to be said.

He has contributed to the book Ready, Aim, Captivate! alongside Deepak Chopra, Ran Zilca, Suzi Pomerantz, Dan Janal, Jim Stovall, and others, and he has his own book on shyness and confidence due out in 2013.

A strong believer that change is always possible, he invites you to *change your mind, change your life.*

Self-confidence, which the dictionary defines as "a feeling of trust in one's abilities, qualities, and judgment," is perhaps the greatest, most important form of confidence that one can have; for the presence of good self-confidence provides a strong foundation for everything we do in life, ranging from the everyday activities in which we find ourselves, all the way to seizing the most rare and powerful of opportunities.

It is not too big a claim to state that strong self-confidence can help you throughout both your personal and your professional lives. Imagine having the confidence to be able to make an excellent first impression on potential new customers and to win their trust, confidence, and business. Imaging how it would feel having the confidence to be able to successfully train people, knowing that you are able to help them get the most from that training and thus make a positive difference to their productivity and their working lives. Picture yourself having the confidence to be able to articulately present your new ideas to the board of directors and hear their positive feedback on a well-presented case! And what would your daily work look like if you had enough self-confidence to be able to handle a meeting with your boss while taking everything in stride, and to be equally productive in your handling of your own team?

All of these situations are much easier to handle when you have a healthy measure of self-confidence underpinning your every action.

Outside of work life, self-confidence can have even more positive results, be it speaking to new people when you are down at the pub with your mates, or meeting new people at parties—heightened self-confidence can work wonders for increasing your circle of friends and, when you get right down to it, can be a wonderful aid in your quest to find "The One"! Now, that's not to say that increased self-confidence is a guarantee of finding your life-partner; however, it is hard to deny that the more self-confident among our friends do tend to be the ones who have the least difficulties on that score. It certainly doesn't harm your chances, and it can make the rest of life so much more enjoyable and productive in the meantime.

So, it is pretty safe to say that at the root of any and all forms of confidence is a strong foundation of self-confidence—when you have strong self-confidence, the rest falls into place so much more easily.

Can Shyness Be Overcome and Self-Confidence Developed?

It is a common misconception that people who are shy are destined to remain shy forever and that all they can do is learn to hide their shyness and pretend to be confident, and that somehow that will get them through life. As any shy person or anyone lacking self-confidence will already know, simply pretending on its own doesn't really get you very far. Sure, it might help for a short while, and you might even fool the people you meet, but inside (where it counts) you still feel as shy as you ever did. Indeed, what can sometimes happen is that you do a great job of fooling others who then refuse to believe that you are shy, which only makes things worse when they force you into uncomfortable situations.

The good news is that it does not have to be like this. I know because I used to be shy. Really shy. Painfully shy in fact! Oh sure, my close friends all thought I was quite an outgoing sort of person, chatty and good fun when out socialising; you probably know what I'm talking about here, right? Because when you are out with your mates, people you've known for a long time, that's one thing. But put me in a situation where I had to speak to strangers, and I would clam up. I used to absolutely hate going to parties, because naturally my mates would go off meeting new people, chatting up girls or boys or both, and pretty soon I'd be left on my own, knowing nobody, and absolutely petrified at the thought of speaking with someone new. What on earth could I say to them? What if they didn't like me? What if they laughed at me?

Have you ever found yourself in that sort of situation? It's awful, isn't it? Or what about seminars through work? I used to love attending them because I'd learn so many new and interesting things (Ok, things other people in other walks of life might find boring, but I enjoyed them), but before you could start, you had to endure the awful "Registration and Coffee" section where you are supposed to stand there and actually talk to complete strangers. People you'd never met before; how on earth could you speak to them? What could you possibly say? So I would be the one stuck in the corner, quietly sipping my tea, urgently studying my shoes, and desperately hoping against hope that nobody would come speak to me. Sound familiar?

I could feel my palms sweating at the thought of speaking to strangers, I would feel scared, sometimes even start to feel physically sick in my stomach. You know, where all you want to do is run in the opposite direction and keep running. Which is exactly what did happen to me one time. I was a member of an online social website (which I'd joined long before Mr. Zuckerberg had even thought of applying to college), where I knew quite a few people and was comfortable chatting with them online. So one year they decided to organise a Christmas party in the real world for us all to get together. How hard could this be? I'd never met them, but I knew them online. It'd be easy, right? You are probably already way ahead of me here! What actually happened was I was in a room full of perfect strangers who I'd never physically met before; I felt the panic rising and, to cut a long story short, I locked myself in the toilet, had a full on twenty-minute panic attack, and then fled, not even pausing to collect my coat from the cloakroom, because that would have meant talking to someone. I ran, and didn't stop running until I was on the train home.

It was then that I decided that I could not go on through life like that anymore. Something had to change. It was time to face up to my shyness and conquer it once and for all.

And I am pleased to say that this is precisely what I proceeded to do. I did a lot of research, became trained in nuerolinguistic programming (NLP) and hypnosis and other cutting-edge sciences, learned how to literally reprogramme my own mind, and set about conquering the shyness that had plagued me for over forty years. With considerable success!

The same online community has Christmas parties each year now, and I went to the most recent one knowing almost nobody there, had a whale of a time, and came away knowing over a dozen new people.

I also went to a new work-related seminar looking forward to the chats at Registration & Coffee, only to be disappointed because the organisers had laid things out with the coffee in the seminar room, so everyone got a coffee and then sat quietly in the chairs waiting for it to start, something that would have delighted the old, shy me but was now frustrating the new, confident me! So instead I randomly selected three people and set myself the challenge of having a chat with each of them, getting their business card, and arranging a follow-up chat, all of which I am happy to say I did.

Furthermore, the confidence I developed as a result of applying my 8 step system has enabled me to fulfill a childhood ambition, that of acting. I now appear in local theatre productions as often as my schedule will allow, and thoroughly enjoy every second of it!

So yes, it really is possible to conquer your shyness and become a much more self-confident person. I have done it myself, and I now help clients all round the world to conquer their shyness.

Why Do Some People Have It and Others Don't?

Why is it that some people seem to have an excess of self-confidence, whereas others are shy, perhaps painfully so?

Why do some people seem to have no problem with speaking to strangers or with standing on stage in front of thousands, whereas you might break into a cold sweat at the thought of speaking to a single person you don't know?

It all boils down to what we learn when we are much younger, typically sometime between zero and seven years of age. That's when we learned all of this, when we learned how to behave with strangers—what we learned then is what guides and controls our behaviour to this very day.

Now, I don't know the exact situations in which you found yourself, nor do I know the experiences you had and the lessons you learned, and it is entirely probably that you are not even aware of them anymore, but they were there, and you learned the lessons the best way you knew how as a young child, and those ways of acting have become ingrained in your subconscious ever since.

The good news is that the fact that you did such a great job of learning how to be shy means that you can do an even better job of learning new and more empowering behaviours, which means that you are perfectly placed to conquer your shyness. Because you did learn those original lessons very well, did you not? This suggests that you are excellent at learning how to behave in different situations, all of which means you have a strong ability to learn these new, more helpful ways to react when you enjoy meeting and talking with strangers, don't you?

There are a number of powerful tools and techniques that I use to help my clients to completely destroy their old shyness, many of which are beyond a single chapter such as this, but the good news is that there are things you can do; if you choose to do them immediately, they will start setting you on the path to loosening the grip your shyness had on you right away, so I'll cover some of these for you right now. Of course, my just writing them does nothing for either of us, which is why you are applying them in your everyday life, because you know that it is through applying these simple tools that you are starting to loosen the grip of your shyness and you are already opening up the doorway to a new and more confident you, aren't you?

Remember when you were young? No, younger than that. The chances are that your parents had a chat with you and said four very important words to you, words that were spoken with the best of intentions and that absolutely served you well. Have you remembered those words yet? "Don't talk to strangers." Yes, those are the words. They were vital when you were a young child, and absolutely the best advice your parents could ever have given you at the time.

But you know what? I bet that nobody, not your parents, teachers, or even yourself, has ever stopped you and taken you to one side and let you know that while those four words were absolutely the right words for you as a young child and that they quite possibly saved you from potential harm and danger when you were young, you are all grown up now and old enough to be able to look after yourself, and that while those words served the young you very well indeed, it is time for you to understand and give yourself permission to know that those words no longer serve your best interests; it is time for you to embrace the fact that now you are grown up, it is ok for you to talk to strangers; indeed it is a vital part of being a grown up that you do talk to strangers and to realise that not only is it ok to talk to strangers but that you can have a lot of fun doing so. In fact, it can lead to some wonderful situations in your life, as you actually enjoy talking to strangers, don't you?

The Biggest Self-Confidence Secret (Perhaps...)

Marie Moseley once said "Never compare your inside to somebody else's outside, because you will always lose," and in doing so revealed one of the most important yet little-known secrets about self-confidence.

Picture the scene. You are back in your school days. It is exam time. You are sitting in the exam hall, and the invigilator tells you all you may now turn over your papers and begin. You start reading the first question. It looks like gibberish. So you move to the next question, which looks like gibberish that has been translated into gobbledegook. And so it goes as you read each of the utterly impossible questions. You wonder how on earth anyone can be expected to answer these questions, and you look around the room at your fellow students, expecting to see equally puzzled stares on their faces. Only, when you look, they all seem to be concentrating on the papers, scribbling away at their undoubtedly perfect answers. Oh no! Everyone else is happy and sailing through this exam, and you are stuck and can't think of any answers and feel awful because you are going to fail and they are all so confident and doing well...

I'm sure we've all been there. I know I have!

Of course, after a while you settle down and reread the questions, and things start to make sense and you begin to answer them, but you can't shake off that feeling that everyone else in the room is doing so much better than you are because they are all scribbling away and they look so sure, so confident.

Sound familiar? I bet it does. And not just in those old exams either!

You see, the problem is that we are comparing how we feel inside with how others look from the outside. And any time anyone on the planet compares how they feel inside with how they think other people look on the outside, they will always lose. For our outside hides much of what we are feeling all the time. Someone can give the outward appearance of being calm and collected and in control, while inside they are a bundle of nerves frantically trying to remember what they are supposed to say next and wondering if anyone will pay attention to them and wishing they were somewhere else entirely!

When you were feeling really nervous in the exam and looking around at all the others who were scribbling away and looking as though they knew exactly what they were doing, what you couldn't see was that inside pretty much most of them had the same sorts of feelings as you—mind in danger of going blank at any second, can't quite remember the full details of the subject, wishing the questions were about a completely different aspect, wondering if they can get it done in time. But, because they are head down over the paper and scribbling away (quite possibly scribbling the only things that come to mind at the time and desperately hoping it will eventually make some sort of point-earning sense), they look as though they are in control. And you know what? If one of them were to look at you as you were scribbling down what little you could dredge up on the topic for the first question, they would almost certainly think "Wow, they know what they are doing, look at them racing through the answers, I bet they do much better than I do."

We all put on a front and hide our true inner feelings with various sorts of masks. We do it all the time, every day, and so does everyone else! That's the key point, which is so important to remember, but which is also oh so easy to forget.

Gary Numan, famous electronic musician, rose to considerable fame in the 1970s especially with his song "Cars." Naturally he and his band played live gigs and appeared on TV. Gary had a very commanding presence on stage, often standing stock still and staring out at the audience, not moving, an impassive expression on his face. People admired his supreme confidence in being able to just stand there in front of everyone and not move—can you imagine how much confidence and courage it would take to stand on stage like that, motionless, lights focused on you, thousands of pairs of eyes all watching you and you alone as you stare out at them? In truth, Gary later revealed, the reason he did this was not because of supreme confidence, it was because he was petrified and couldn't think what else to do, so he pretty much froze! So while the audience and critics were admiring this supremely confident young man totally in control of his emotions and feelings, he was actually standing there petrified, mind blank, unable to think what to do. Quite a difference between his inside and his outside!

How does this relate to you and your shyness or your lack of self-confidence?

By simply remembering that you should never compare your inside to somebody else's outside, because you will always lose, you can start to realise that you may not be as shy as you fear you are, and that those supremely-confident people around you are almost certainly not all as confident as they appear.

So next time you are at that party or networking event or seminar gathering or in the pub waiting for your friends, and you feel awkward and out of place because everyone else looks as though they fit in, remember that the only person in the room whose true feelings you can know are your own, and remember that we all generally look a lot calmer on the outside than we ever feel inside. That person standing there on their own, looking as though they are totally calm and without a care in the world—chances are they are as nervous and as shy as you are and far from rebuffing any advances and would almost certainly be thoroughly grateful if you went up to them and said hello and started chatting. They are probably looking at you thinking "Wow, I wish I was as calm and confident as they are!

Three Steps to Develop Your Self-Confidence

Here are three steps you can use to continue the development of your own self-confidence as you work to conquer your shyness and build new and more empowering ways of behaving with people.

1. Know Your Good Points
"It's not vanity to know your own good points. It would just be stupidity if you didn't. It's only vanity when you get puffed up about them." –L. M. Montgomery.

All too often, too many of us are told to hide our light under a bushel, to not let people know at what we excel, for fear of being perceived as boasting. At first glance, that seems like a reasonable idea—after all, rare is the person who likes people who boast about how fantastic they are. Many of us can recall with a sense of dread those encounters with the pub bore or the office bore or the party bore, who corners you at every opportunity and goes on and on about their talents. We don't want to be that person, so we heed strongly the advice to hide our skills, be modest, and not make a fuss, when we are good at something or even the expert.

This avoids our risking being the vainglorious bore, true enough.

But it brings with it a significant risk of its own, one that can ultimately cause us even more damage in the long run. That risk is that we can get to be so good at hiding away our talents, skills, and expertise from others, we can end up hiding them away from ourselves too. And by doing that, we ensure that we artificially limit ourselves, limiting what we can achieve, and denying ourselves the opportunity to fulfill our true potential.

I remember back when I was studying and training to be a presenter and speaker: I'd done a fair amount of training, and I could create and present talks, even receive standing ovations in some cases. But no matter how well I'd done, my need to ensure that I wasn't boasting about my abilities meant that I tell myself that I was not a very good speaker, that I was a poor presenter, and that I was nowhere near as good as my peers. This really came to a head during an advanced training session I was attending along with my peers and equals. So determined was I to avoid inflating my own sense of importance that I had suppressed knowledge of my abilities even from my own conscious. So convinced was I, as a result, that I was inferior to my peers, that the inevitable finally happened: during one exercise I lost myself completely to my insecurities and froze during my presentation. My mind went completely blank, I was totally lost as to what I was supposed to be doing, and my frantic pleas to my mind to give me something, anything, were met with a simple "No, I got nothing, I told you we weren't good enough!" I froze for what felt like hours (but was in reality five to ten seconds) before my mind took pity on me and gave me something.

I was discussing what had happened with some of my fellow students afterwards, explaining that I just did not think I was that good.

Their reactions stunned me, as they reminded me of all the successful presentations I have done, pointing out how good I actually really am at speaking and presenting, and wondering what on earth I was on about when I called myself "not good enough."

All this got me to thinking that if they believe I am good enough, and the evidence all shows that I am more than good enough, why did I not believe it myself? I worked on it overnight, applying some neat little mind-training tools to help me sort myself out (the same kind which I successfully use with my coaching clients), and I resumed the advanced training course the next day with a new mindset—knowing what I can do, aware of my skills and strengths, understanding what I'm good at. And I have to say, my presentations since have been all the better for it because, not wishing to boast, I am good at speaking and presenting, just like my peers and fellow students on the advanced course.

You may well have found yourself in situations where you felt you couldn't do something or didn't know something, and yet people around you were sure that you could do it or did know it. Or worse and more harmfully, you may have found yourself, say, up for promotion to a position for which you are actually well suited, but your modesty and reserved approach meant that you even convinced yourself that you weren't good enough and so you missed out on the opportunity, which should have been yours for the taking.

When we hide our skills and abilities even from ourselves, we are not serving anyone—we are actually denying people who may need the benefit of our skills as well as limiting our own progress, perhaps one of the most selfish things we can do!

So why don't you take a moment, right now to pause and reflect upon what you can do. What things are you actually good at despite telling yourself you are not? And what might you be able to do in life if you stopped hiding your abilities from yourself? What has such hiding cost you already?

So go on, while it's fresh in your mind, list fifty things you are actually good at even though you might be telling yourself you aren't. Then for each one write a couple of sentences about how you know you are good at it, and how knowing this is going to change things for you for the better in some way—it doesn't have to be a massive change; it could be some small effect, but it all builds up.

Then next time you find yourself thinking "I can't do this," check your list to see if you really can't, or if you are just sabotaging your ability to shine brightly.

2. Celebrate!

"Acrobat: The only person who can do what everyone else would like to do—pat themselves on the back." –Anon

Most of us know how helpful it is to congratulate someone on a job well done. Whether it is a huge job or a much smaller endeavor, the act of taking a moment to acknowledge their achievement and to let them know their efforts did not go unnoticed is a very powerful one; it can make the recipient feel the little bit more appreciated, more empowered, and can make everything seem worthwhile in that moment. Most of us also know how good it feels when someone does the same to us, patting us on the back when we complete something. It feels good, doesn't it, to know that your hard work was not in vain. And it can even help to strengthen the relationship between the two people, knowing that they appreciate you and vice versa.

But there is someone who pretty much all of us will never take the time to stop and congratulate, no matter how sterling a job they do. And there is also someone who, no matter how much effort we put in, will never seem to be pleased enough with us, because they will never ever thank us, let alone congratulate us.

This is a big shame and, when you think about it, a problem, because it's those little moments of interaction, of bonding, of appreciation, which can make a huge difference to our day and, in the long run, to our lives; that acknowledgement and recognition feels so uplifting, doesn't it?

I used to go through life, as most of us do, with a huge, overflowing (and regularly filling) in-tray of things I had to do, tasks I needed to complete, and problems all in need of my attention. I'd do my best on each one, getting them done to the best of my ability, but I'd often end up getting more and more stressed, because as soon as I finished one thing, I'd see that metaphorical in-tray of life with so many other things, which all needed doing, the pile never seeming to get any smaller, and I'd start beating myself up over not getting things done fast enough as I plunged into the next thing I had to do. Many of you are reading this and nodding in self-recognition right now, I'd be willing to bet! And it's a stressful place to be, isn't it? But just imagine if, upon completing a task and before rushing on to the next one, you had taken just a moment to pause and pat yourself on the back, and even celebrate a job well done. You know how good it feels when someone else congratulates you; imagine how even more empowering it feels when the person who knows you best does it? It even strengthens your own relationship with yourself.

It's a simple step, isn't it? Yet it can have a profound effect on you.

Why not think of a way in which you could celebrate with yourself when you've completed something? You don't have to wait until it's a huge task; even smaller tasks deserve that moment to pause, celebrate, and pat yourself on the back. So how might you celebrate? A small inward word of gratitude, perhaps? Punching the air? Singing a few bars of a celebratory song? It doesn't matter what it is; the important thing is that it works for you, and that you do it every time.

So, take a moment here to think about how you are going to celebrate your successes from now on, and resolve right here to become the person who is grateful for all you do, the person who recognises what a great job you do, the person who is always there to help you celebrate checking off that to-do list entry. Decide to do this from now on and commit to doing this every time you complete something.

Once you've chosen your celebratory ritual and made the commitment to unleash your inner acrobat by doing it every time, pat yourself on the back and celebrate having completed the task of making that decision right now.

Feels good, doesn't it?

3. Going from Small Talk Killer to Killer Small Talk.

"'My idea of good company, Mr Elliot, is the company of clever, well-informed people, who have a great deal of conversation; that is what I all good company.' 'You are mistaken', said he gently, 'that is not good company, that is the best'"–Jane Austen, Persuasion

Oh how right they are. Great company with sparkling flowing conversation—it's hard to beat it. And once you are in that zone, with the conversation flowing freely, it is easy to contribute one's own observations and experiences, especially when the topic turns to something one enjoys.

But we never find ourselves magically in the middle of such conversations: they all have to start somewhere, i.e the dreaded "Small Talk."

Who likes small talk? Certainly there are some people who naturally relish the chance to partake, but for the vast majority, small talk is something to be avoided whenever possible. It is scary, nerve-wracking, and generally, nobody knows what to say. And it's not just us "ordinary" people who fear it; it seems that even the big-league players, VPs of multinational companies who think nothing of holding court in high-power business meetings, find themselves floundering like a child when it comes to social chit-chat and small talk.

You know what it's like. You are in a room, perhaps at a party or maybe a pre-seminar coffee room at registration. You see someone and feel you ought to chat, but you can't think of anything to say other than "hello" and "what brings you here" (probably the same thing that brings you here, obviously!), so you miss out on the opportunity. Or you do go up to them and have a scintillating conversation along the lines of

You: "Hello." Them: "Hello." You: "So, where are you from?" Them: "London, you?" You: "Manchester."

At this point the conversation dies as you can't think of what to say, so you drift away to the next person and repeat the same soul-destroying process over and over again.

If only there was a way of livening up that opening conversation without it sounding like you are launching into a well-rehearsed monologue or grilling them in an interview.

Ah, but there is a way. It requires a little bit of work on your part in advance, but once you've done that work, it will serve you for many conversations to come.

Why does the conversation opener above fail? Because neither one of you knows anything about the other (yet), you have no common framework, don't know of any common interests, and the short conversation gives no clues—you both literally have nothing to talk about because neither of you gives the other any topics topics to discuss. And as we typically only allow a precious few moments to see if a conversation will develop, with nothing to talk about the conversation is doomed from the outset.

So what if, instead of giving closed answers, we offer more open answers; responses with a little bit more meat to them, which the other person can then use as a conversational springboard?

Them: "Hello." You: "Hello." Them: "So, where are you from?" You: "I'm from Nowheresville, it's a small village, but it was one of the main producers of widgets at the turn of the century and has the oldest pub in the country. How about you?"

You've just given the other person several juicy chunks, which they can use to build the conversation—it might move to talking about life in villages or widgets or pubs or history, which gives plenty of scope for conversation.

I recall a networking event I was attending in the bar after a seminar. The evening was wearing on, and I was thinking about heading home, having had about as many forced-yet-fruitless conversations as I could handle for the night, when a delegate I'd not spoken to before said hello. We quickly introduced ourselves, and he asked where I was from. Noting that he had a hint of a Scottish accent and held in his hand a glass of what could well have been whisky, I responded that I'm originally from a small village called Aberlour in the heart of Malt Whisky country—indeed from my old bedroom window I could see the Macallan distillery across the valley. Turns out my guess about the contents of his glass was right and my answer lead us into a wonderful, long, wide-ranging and productive conversation. Now, had I not seen his whisky glass nor detected his accent, I'd have probably opted for a different nugget of information about my hometown, or I might not even have mentioned where I'd grown up but instead mentioned where I live now.

You see, as helpful as the extra information you slip in may be, it has to be relevant—after all, it has to be something that can spark off a conversation, which means it has to have a good chance of being vaguely relevant to the person you are speaking with. You can't just use the same stock answer for all occasions and hope to impress; you need to use the right hook for the job, which is where a little bit of research on your part in advance will reap dividends for months and years to come.

What do you know, right now, about your hometown? If someone asked you to list ten interesting facts about where you are from, could you do it? Possibly, although the vast majority of us would struggle after about three or four items at the most. And if we are struggling to come up with interesting facts in the calm and comfort of reading this article, imagine how much harder it is to think of them when faced with a new conversation?

This is why the effort you are about to spend on a little bit of research will be so worthwhile, as it will enable you to slip in relevant little snippets as circumstances arise. As with any research, there are a wide variety of sources open to you including, naturally, the Internet, but also (depending upon the place you have in mind) other sources such as tourist information, local newspapers, local business associations, and even estate agents.

Have a good look around and come up with at least ten different interesting snippets of information about your hometown (or your company or your business—or even ten on each!), gems you could easily slip into your answer to "Where are you from?" in order to get the conversation going. Make sure they cover different topics and include as wide a selection as possible, because you are going to need to rely upon these to help you to be prepared for all eventualities. And once you have your list of ten interesting facts, memorise them—you will need to be able to recall them and slip them in effortlessly, so a little extra preparation at this stage will help you from being stuck in small talk to being known as a well-informed person with whom others enjoy great conversation!

Congratulations!

You have now read and learned several important steps, which are already, through your application of them right now, taking you on the journey towards strong self-confidence and conquering your shyness.

The more you reread, learn, and apply these points, the stronger your new foundations will become.

It is traditional at this point to list the key points we've covered together as well as the lessons learned for easy reference.

However, I am not going to do that, because doing so would rob you of many valuable learning experiences, for these are not lessons best learned by being told, but rather by reading, rereading, studying, delving into and discovering for yourself. There are many useful lessons within this chapter, some you may find easy to spot, and others you may not discover until you have reread it a few times, started using the tools, and reflected upon what you've discovered; those are going to be the most empowering lessons of all, and that is precisely why I do not intend to deprive you of them by crudely listing them now!

You are now already in possession of some of the tools I give to my clients when we work together—may you find them as useful a foundation as my successful clients do throughout their lives!

Intimacy and Sex: The Twin Pillars of an Intimate Relationship

by Graham Phoenix

Graham is the founder of Male eXperience, a site about men, masculinity, and sexuality. He teaches men how to become aware of their strength and how to understand women so they can experience their male energy, love their partner, and create a relationship of love and passion.

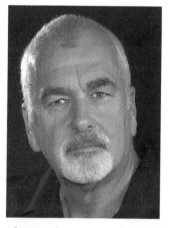

He helps men embrace what is within them, waiting to be released. He encourages them to drop the mask and create their "Personal Masculinity" though change and growth. Through his work men become aware of themselves, present, open to change, and embrace new approaches.

His online program, "How To Love A Woman," takes men on a journey that enables them to become aware of their issues, to face their life and design it the way they desire it to be. It enables them to look anew at their relationship and recreate it so they can live a new life with their partner. It is designed to help men become the man that can love their woman. It is the first step on a journey that will transform their life and the life of their partner or future partner.

Participants will be challenged to become a man who can be strong in himself at the same time as love a woman, in short, a man who can be with a woman.

The course covers three major, basic issues that affect men:

How to discover and develop the man inside.
How to understand and appreciate women.
How to love their woman.

Women look for depth in a man. They look for a man who is grounded and strong in himself. The course seeks to help men create that.

He used to work internationally as a lighting designer and now lives in Spain where he writes. He still speaks and mentors internationally.

Intimacy and sex touch the core of any intimate relationship and are the twin pillars that support it. However, many men have issues or problems with intimacy and sex that often result in relationship breakdown. Unsurprisingly, this area is where there is much confusion between men and women.

I am a man and I write from a male perspective for men. This does not mean that I write to be confrontational, in fact, quite the opposite: I write to bring men and women together but with an emphasis on how men need to look at the situation, how men need to change.

On this journey we are making together I look at a number of issues that focus on intimacy. In considering love, the focus is on how to love your partner. If you develop this ability to love, you will earn the undying love of your woman. Talking about emotional relationships, I show that man who understands intimacy, a man who understands love, a man who understands and can have an emotional relationship is a powerful man that will be loved because he can love.

Shifting the focus to sex I look at how to build sexual polarity with your partner. This is a vital ingredient in improving a relationship. One of the reasons that sex fades is that there isn't sufficient polarity between the partners. There is a modern emphasis on equality that, unfortunately, can also be wrongly interpreted in a personal sense. I consider your physical relationship. This involves both of you in a relationship of equal responsibility. As the man, you can lead your partner, but the result does depend on two-way communication.

Attraction

Men start with attraction and find they're attracted to women. They realise later that having been attracted, they haven't worked out how to love that woman, but they want to, and they want the relationship to grow and become powerful.

A relationship is where you discover something important. You discover how different women are from men. It's not enough to just be with a woman. Men bond, men can be in silence together, men can drink or watch sports together, and do nothing else. Women are not the same. As a man, you discover that you need to bring more to a relationship. Being the sexy, interesting man that created the attraction in the first place is not enough. You need to be more of a man inside. You need to be stronger, more powerful, and more compassionate.

Women look for more in you. Women look for real depth in a man, so once you're beyond that first stage of attraction, that first powerful jolt of sexual polarity, women look for depth. They look for a man who's grounded, a man who's strong in himself, a man who knows who he is and where he's going, a man who knows his passion in life, a man who's focused and directed.

Men seek to know who they are and what their place is in the world. Men wonder how they can get their power back and want to create relationships of strength and compassion.

Intimacy

If your relationship has lost its excitement and passion then this will help you re-discover it. Passion and excitement are always high when you first meet a woman and fall in love, but you may well have experienced them dying.

This is for you if you have difficulty being intimate with your partner and difficulty admitting this. Here I'm talking about emotional intimacy. Many men have difficulty being intimate with their partners.

If your understanding of intimacy differs from your partner's and you don't know how to move forward, the answers are here. It's important to learn what your understanding of intimacy is versus that of your partner. You both need to understand each other and be on the same page. Intimacy, emotional intimacy, is important to women. They start with emotions. Emotions are where they live, but men tend to miss this.

If you create a deep relationship of power, passion, and intimacy, it will affect far more than just your relationship. It will affect everything you do in your life. It will enable you to create success in your business, in all of your working life. It will allow the passion in your life to flow, because when your relationship is amazing, you are amazing. Your life will have excitement and passion because that's what your woman wants to see. She wants a man with excitement, passion, direction, and masculinity.

The simple truth is that men often, I would say frequently, have issues with intimacy, and what compounds this is that they're frequently unable to admit that they have these issues. It's this combination that causes such angst, such frustration, such confusion in women. They see men sublimating their emotions in actions such as work, drinking, fishing, or sports.

This is at the heart of much of the difficulty between men and women. For men it starts with sex, not intimacy, and for women it starts with intimacy, not sex. That's a major conflict, a confusion between men and women, which has been going on throughout time. It will probably carry on. I would love to think that all men would read a book such as this and resolve these issues in their lives, but I think the sad truth is that they won't. Not all men have that determination to make their lives intimate and connected.

Intimacy is being close to someone on an emotional level to the point where you feel that you start to merge together. It's often associated with a close sexual relationship, and this is where men find it confusing. Women almost always connect intimacy with an emotional state that can lead to sex. Men connect intimacy with an emotional state that follows sex.

What is intimacy? It's a vulnerable sharing of inner thoughts, feelings, spirit, and true self, and it's achieved through listening, empathy, or reassurance. If it's mutual, it results in feeling known, validated, and cared for. When you to talk to your partner, listen to her, tell her you love her; when you make her feel known, validated, and cared for; when you are empathetic and reassure her, that's intimacy.

Men often confuse sex and intimacy, but they are not the same thing. Sex without intimacy can be very unrewarding, while sex with intimacy can be deeply passionate and fulfilling. This can be difficult for men to understand. Men are so focused on the power of the sexual act that they often miss the intimacy, but even then, they know that it's just a physical act and not a passionate or fulfilling one.

Men see intimacy as a deep physical connection and focus on understanding each other's physical needs, but women see intimacy as deep emotional connection. For them it's the ability to understand each other's emotional needs and share emotional moments. It's that sharing, that deep involvement in emotional moments from the depth of your relationship.

Masculine identity masks the need for intimacy in men. Intimacy involves tenderness, compassion, empathy. They're feelings associated with the feminine, and they cause men to avoid intimacy in their minds. Intimacy is often seen as threatening to men's gender identity. Men don't like that. They don't like to be considered emotional or weak, so they avoid it.

Intimacy requires uniting with another person, so for a man it can be seen as endangering themselves through a loss of control, a loss of identity. It is important for a man to retain control, control over himself and his identity. Intimacy blurs the edges that separate him from a woman. That can be difficult.

Men avoid intimacy because they lack the emotional vocabulary. They feel less able to express the way they're feeling and feel uncomfortable discussing emotions. But it is a skill that can be learned. It's a skill you need to keep on learning and developing because intimacy creates an experience of emotional closeness in a relationship. It's not just two people living together. It's two people merging on a deep emotional level. It's two people able to emotionally open with one another and reveal their true feelings, thoughts, fears, and desires.

Have you revealed your true feelings to your partner? Has she revealed hers to you? If not, you need to get on with it, and you need to find a way of doing it without frightening or threatening her. Do it by enclosing her, drawing her in, involving her, caring for her. Intimacy creates a bond that is hard to break and strengthens a relationship.

When intimacy is lacking, there can be an experience of loneliness for both partners. It is one of the universal human needs, the need to have someone acknowledge you, to validate you, recognize you, know you exist and know how you feel. The lack of intimacy is one of the commonest reasons for relationship breakdown. It is the issue that is dealt with over and over and over again in relationships that are falling apart.

When the initial passion of a relationship disappears, it may seem to lose its intensity. It signals the beginning of a new phase in which both partners need to invest effort to maintain the emotional closeness that seemed to come so effortlessly early on. It was effortless, but now it seems you need to make an effort.

Love

I have learned how to love a woman and how to put it into practice. Love and intimacy are forever entwined. To learn one is to learn the other.

There are some simple steps you can take to create intimacy and love in your relationship. With your new understanding of what intimacy is, you'll see that they're both involved. There are seven simple steps, ones that you can put into practice every day of your life. Write them down, pin them up, and never forget them.

1. Tell her you love her. It means saying it so that she completely understands and is in no doubt about it. She needs you to say this all the time, to volunteer it and not say it in reply to her questioning.

2. Just love her for herself. You know the qualities that you love in her; maybe she is smart, sexy, inspirational, funny, or even rich. This is not why you love her. You love her just because of her and nothing else. Even though you celebrate everything that she is, even though you worship her for what she does in the world, she needs to know that you simply love her, no matter what.

3. Get to know her. How often do you hear men say, "My wife doesn't understand me?" What that really means is "I don't understand my wife." This is basic in learning how to love a woman. Love can only grow and deepen through understanding. You'll never get to the point where you know everything about her. No woman is

that simple. She is a complex person that even she doesn't understand.

4. Count your blessings. This means the blessings you have together, the things you've achieved together, all that you are as a couple. It should be a regular part of your life together. While you shouldn't live in the past, it's okay to recount the great things in the past, but this must be tempered by looking at the amazing things that you're going to do in the future.

5. Give love always. Love is about giving rather than receiving. Love is a creative force that grows out of the desire to give more than you receive. It's crucial that you are able to receive the love that is offered to you, otherwise it quickly dies, but you have to focus on the contribution you make to her.

6. Pay attention to her. It's a truth that women need attention all the time. It's absolutely vital that all men wanting to know how to love a woman understand this. Many of the annoying habits that women have are merely attempts to get the attention of a man who is not paying her any attention. Take heed of them and pay attention.

7. Start afresh each day. This is what I do. Start your day as if it was your first day of your relationship. Welcome her into your world and look forward to your day together. Give her your love and tell her you love her. Do it again in a different way and repeat. I'm sure I don't have to tell you where to go from here. This refreshing of your love will keep it alive and bring you closer to each other. Through this, your love will deepen and become an essential part of every day you spend together. Start tomorrow morning. Start as if it were your first day of your relationship.

Emotional Relationships

In an emotional relationship, two people have such deep feelings for each other that even during tough times they will know that they are connected together. This emotional connection keeps them strong. When they share emotional intimacy, others cannot intervene and disrupt their relationship. With such a bond there is no place for misunderstandings or conflict.

Truth, honesty, and faithfulness are the main pillars of any emotional relationship. When two people love deeply, their relationship always grows and develops. When love is bonded with emotions, the relationship is powerful. Communicating your emotions to your partner will make her feel loved, because it confirms that you understand her needs and desires.

What can be extremely threatening to a relationship is an emotional affair. An emotional affair is when you turn to someone else for your core emotional support. It can develop slowly, even innocently, as a friendship. There may not be a sexual attraction in this budding friendship. But when your relationship is experiencing conflict or distance, and you pull away from your partner, consistently turning to your "friend" for support and sharing of deep personal matters, an emotional affair has begun.

An emotional affair can be a great source of relief and comfort during relationship difficulties. But the danger is that there is only so much intimate emotional energy to go around. When you begin to invest significant amounts of your emotional energy in someone else, your relationship can be seriously compromised.

An emotional affair can deepen through constant contact. There becomes an excitement in hearing from the other person, and when it leads to physical intimacy, it's often a little sex and a lot of talking. The sex may be intense and passionate, but it is the feeling of emotional safety and companionship that really fuels the bond at the deepest level.

This friendship can doom your relationship. Once the door of emotional intimacy has been opened and the bond deepens, you cannot help but compare. "It's so easy to talk to her, and so hard to talk to my partner" is the common refrain. "She always complains and criticises, but my friend is always there, always in a good mood, and always understands and listens to me." It is much easier to open up and feel safe in a superficial, new friendship compared to a long-term, committed relationship.

Sex

Many relationships start with passion and great sex but then drift into a sense of indifference where sex is concerned. Age, stress, children all combine to interfere with either your, or your partner's, sexual performance. This is, for obvious reasons, most noticeable in a man, and, as a result, causes most concern in a man. Once sex ceases to be so prominent, you both have to fall back on friendship or companionship. Many couples are not set up to function well at these levels.

The answer to this is two-fold. At one level working on the emotional bond between you can reap enormous rewards, as we have already seen. At another level, rejuvenating sex in your relationship becomes critical. There are a number of issues to be dealt with in order to do this, but I would hope that, if this is an issue you face, some of what you have been learning here will contribute to the new atmosphere needed.

The quality of sex in a relationship can be seen as a marker for the quality of the relationship. Improving the sex will improve the relationship, but also improving the relationship will improve the sex. It is a classic chicken and egg dilemma: where to start? I feel that it should always be with the relationship.

If you have sexual performance issues with your partner, it is time to resolve these. If there is a lack of sexual polarity in your relationship you need to understand that developing polarity with your partner is crucial. Understanding the role of sex in your relationship will ensure this area grows and develops.

One of the big issues in the media around the subject of gender is how men use their sexuality. The stereotypical complaint is that they use it to dominate women, that there is too much sexualisation by men. Men can see themselves as Alpha Males who have a right to use whatever technique they can to acquire and enjoy women, i.e. men can physically dominate women to make themselves feel like a man. Most men, however, either don't quite understand their sexuality or feel threatened by the danger of abusing women.

Men can feel caught between the need to be men and the perception of abuse. Either way, it stems from the man's lack of certainty about himself and his ability to deal with male sexuality and polarity. Male sexuality is a potent force that needs to be understood and integrated as part of a man's personality rather than simply controlled. Suppressing it creates dangerous power than can easily cause harm.

The everyday truth, though, is that many men have difficulties in their physical relationships. Despite the talk of male sexual dominance, in a relationship, the opposite is frequently the problem. Sexual dominance is a characteristic more of single men or men outside their relationship. Inside a relationship, we find a different picture.

For a man to be potent is for him to be strong and powerful and fully in charge of the sexuality in his physical relationship. This is the ideal, but how can it be achieved along with the daily stress of living with your partner?

As a relationship develops, the level of sexuality changes. This is normal. But since intense sexual attraction is usually an important bonding element early in a relationship, sexual changes often seem unwelcome. Many factors are involved in these changes.

One of the most fundamental challenges is the decline in sexual novelty. Novelty is a major sexual stimulant. Novelty was probably automatic early in your relationship, but later, sex naturally became more familiar and less novel.

Low desire is the top sexual problem in relationships. For men, the top complaint is low frequency, although many women share this concern; for women, the top complaint is quality, or rather lack of it. You may need to find ways to increase the stimulation of your sex life to compensate for the loss of this novelty.

Other common interfering factors in sex include anger, time, avoidance, and anxiety.

While most couples don't want to make love while they are in the middle of a fight, it's a mistake to put aside your sex life for an extended period because of disagreements. Repair your fights and don't interrupt your sex life out of anger. In my first marriage, I withdrew from sex out of anger at what was happening between us. That had a disastrous effect on our relationship.

Lack of time is one of the most commonly cited reasons for infrequency of sex. One of the most common myths is that sex has to take a certain amount of time. Of course, leisurely sex can be wonderful, but it's a luxury that few couples can afford on a regular basis. There is nothing wrong with quickie sex, as long as both partners accept it.

A top myth is that sex must be spontaneous. It's a fact of modern life that we plan and schedule everything that is a priority, so make sex a priority and include it in your schedule. Date night is popular with many couples, but some experts advocate planning frequent, very brief sexual encounters.

Anxiety is a frequent interfering factor. Sometimes anxiety is related to inhibitions acquired earlier in life. Performance is a big source of anxiety—performance used to be a male concern, but now women, too, feel pressure to perform sexually. It's hard for mere mortals to live up to the sexual expectations and images promoted by the media.

Sex is an important bonding component in relationships, so even if you feel somewhat alienated from your partner, sex can often be the experience that restores your bond. It can allow you both to feel closer, get affection, and stimulate a sense of intimacy. For some men who don't talk very much in relationships, sex can help them open up a little. Sex can prime the pump for intimacy and healing, although intimacy should be thought of as separate from sex.

Self-esteem and sexual desire go hand-in-hand. You have to take care of yourself physically, so you feel good about yourself, in order to feel desirable. A new exercise program, taking off a few pounds, being active, and getting enough sleep will all help increase your sex drive.

Couples need to be honest with each other about what they find desirable. If you've been together a long time, your desires will evolve, too. Maybe you'll want erotica or sex toys, for example.

Take turns initiating sex. Take turns being in total control while your partner remains totally passive. These strategies help to deal with common complaints that partners take too little or too much responsibility. Polarity reversal can be an exciting stimulant if it is consensual.

Sex is not rocket science, which means anyone can be good at it, and you can keep improving your skills. In fact, getting better at sex is part of your job, because good sex is part of the foundation of a good relationship.

You can start by talking to your partner more. In addition to talking about sex and sharing your sexual fantasies, you and your partner should talk more in general. Improving your communication and talking to one another more frequently will make you feel closer to one another. This will make you more intimate and probably less inhibited when it comes to sex.

There is a connection in most couples between happiness and having sex. Happy couples have more sex, and the more sex a couple has, the happier they report being. But keep in mind that sex is only one form of intimacy, and that some couples are fairly happy (and intimate) without sex.

Sexual Polarity

Polarity, when talking about people, is the state and control of masculine and feminine energy. In general, a high level of masculine energy will attract women, and a high level of feminine energy will attract men.

A person with more polarity will generally stand out and be more attractive to the opposite sex. If a man shows a feminine polarity and a woman shows a masculine polarity, their polarity and sexual attraction can still exist, but if their polarity is suppressed, the sexual attraction decreases.

A conscious control of polarity can help you become more attractive. But despite high degrees of polarity, men and women retain the essence of male and female qualities, reflecting the true nature of who they really are.

If men and women cling to sameness in masculine or feminine energy, in moments of intimacy, sexual attraction disappears. Quite simply, the juice of the sexual attraction dries up. Love may still be strong, friendship may still be strong, but sexual polarity fades, unless in moments of intimacy one partner is willing to play the masculine pole and the other is willing to play the feminine. You have to animate the masculine and feminine differences if you want to have sexual passion.

You can have a loving friendship between two people with similar polarity, but when you want strong sexual polarity, you need a more masculine and feminine partner.

Physical Relationships

In the last fifty years, gender roles have changed dramatically, adding confusion to our expectations, yet the biology of sexuality and the innate physical, mental, and emotional differences between men and women have not changed in thousands of years, and it is not likely that they will dramatically change anytime soon.

In his fascinating book, What Could He Be Thinking?, Michael Gurian describes the science behind the differences between men and women, which is reflected in how their brains function. Much of the mystery can be dispelled when we understand that male and female brains operate very differently from one another, and that our hormones dictate much of our behavior, both physically and emotionally.

When processing emotions, far more areas of the brain were active in women's brains than in men's. The female brain has 15 percent more blood flow than the male brain, with more neural pathways connecting different parts of the brain, simultaneously engaging parts of the brain that are not stimulated in men.

Men are more capable of spatial skills, including mechanical design, measurement, direction, abstraction, and manipulation of physical objects, while women are more verbally skilled than men. Studies show that men use about half the amount of words that women do. Women love to talk about their emotions, while for most men, talking about their emotions is often difficult and even stressful.

Men tend to react to a perceived threat with a physical response, while women will try to talk themselves out of a stressful situation.

During sex a woman tends to bond intensely with her partner, creating romantic attachment. About the only time a man reacts in the same way is during orgasm allowing him to bond with his partner. However, after orgasm, this reduces in a man, while the woman's capacity remains consistently high. This is why a man may be compelled to say, "I love you" during sex, but may not feel like saying it much afterwards when the woman is longing to hear reassuring words of love and affection.

Much of the more aggressive, sexual, and action-oriented responses in men are caused by high secretions of testosterone. A man's system is dominated by testosterone, with twenty times more of this hormone than is found in a woman's system. In women, testosterone levels usually increase only around the time of ovulation, causing interest in sexual bonding.

Deep in the limbic system of the brain, where our primal urges reside, lies the amygdala, which handles many of our emotions and aggressive tendencies. The amygdala is larger in men than in women, leading to increased aggression.

The feminine, that is the energy which resides in the female brain, is pure, boundless, and with infinite energy, moving freely without any particular direction. It is directionless but immense, ever changing, beautiful, and destructive, the force of life and source of inspiration. The feminine moves in all directions, while the masculine moves in one direction. The feminine needs the masculine to give it direction, focus and purpose, while the masculine needs the energy of the feminine to give it drive and passion. In short, the masculine and the feminine need each other. The masculine directs while the feminine projects. This is the relationship of yin and yang.

The feminine looks to the masculine for direction. A woman does not want a man to look to her for direction; she'd rather he follow his own direction. It is better for a man to act when he wants to and not need a woman to give him permission. A woman would rather a man acts when he chooses instead of when she desires it, and for him to be able to change her feelings at will. That is why a woman prefers a man to take the initiative in everything. She wants him to keep leading and advancing every step of the way instead of waiting for a sign, not without knowing what to do next.

My wife and I experienced something recently that revealed to us previously hidden depths to our relationship. We had begun a close and passionate relationship that we both enjoyed. The one aspect, however, that secretly gave us both concern was that we had never experienced the dark side of each other's nature. There is normally a point in any relationship where you discover the dark side of your partner's nature. Usually when this occurs, it creates confusion or concern as you have uncovered something that is not in line with how you saw your partner.

Most people never think about this and are shocked when it comes out. Both my wife and I had previous marriages that ended in divorce. We were both married to partners who had addictive natures, and we both stayed in our marriages because we thought we could help them solve their addictions. Eventually we both left our marriages, but only after we realized we were enabling the addictions rather than curing them. Entering into a new relationship we both feared what might be lurking in the other. We didn't talk about it, but each knew the other's concerns.

Somehow we knew that we had to experience each other's dark side. We knew we had to resolve this before we went too deeply into the relationship—we had to find out. But how? How could we be sure we knew if we did find out?

We were in India spending some time at an Ashram. Towards the end of our visit, we both independently signed up for a three-day meditation class. We attended the class and worked with various partners. On the last day the teacher announced that we would do a dark energy meditation, one that would, if we engaged with it, delve the depths of our dark side. We immediately opted to do this together, each sensing that the other felt a simultaneous sense of excitement and dread about doing it.

The intention of the meditation was simply to provoke one another and see how far we could go, but the experience would transform our relationship into one of total trust and knowledge.

We started by sitting across from each other, spending time becoming completely present with each other, while tuning out the other people in the room. The meditation was to be energetic and physical. We started to pull faces and make gestures to try and provoke each other. Over a period of ten to fifteen minutes we moved to a form of play fighting. We were feeling each other out, sensing where the other person was and seeing how far we could go.

Eventually the play fighting stopped, and we became serious. We were fighting, wrestling, to such an extent that the teacher came over to make sure we were ok. She was concerned about how far we were going. Once she was sure we knew what we were doing, she let us carry on. Eventually we collapsed on the ground, hugging and laughing. We had broken through a barrier, and we both felt truly amazing.

What I need to explain is what happened energetically when we started really fighting. Physically I am larger and stronger than my wife, and I knew I could wipe the floor with her if I let go of any restraint. My wife knew this, but she didn't know whether I would lose my restraint if she pushed me far enough. She also didn't know if I would just bow out in fear of hurting her. For her, the latter would be almost as bad as the former.

So she pushed and provoked. She pushed harder and harder to test my reaction. I felt this and saw that she was serious about it. I responded by always topping what she did, but only just. I never let her beat me, but I only did enough to ensure she knew I wasn't going to back down. At one point I threw her on the floor and hurt her, but that didn't stop her. She realised that I wasn't going to back down, but neither was I going to lose my temper, something she knew had been my habit in the past. In matching her aggression, I was also protecting her. I was letting her do what she wanted but making sure she knew she would get it back.

Eventually she gave up, knowing there was no further she could go. I could hold her and stop her and give as good as I got. We were very happy because we discovered each other's dark side. I knew she would go as far as she could, take what I gave back, and not take it personally. She knew I would take whatever she gave me, give her back more, but not lose my temper or restraint. I would always remain strong and protect her. I would not back down but would remain, for her, a man.

None of this was planned or talked about as we did it—we followed our instincts and allowed ourselves to go deep into our dark energy. This was what we wanted and it cleared any doubt between us. It was important to us that this was a physical exercise. It had a deep sexual undertone even though sex did not appear in it. It's important that you understand how sex can be involved in a physical relationship even when there is no sexual activity.

The Way Forward

I believe that as men we are all born with a built-in masculine essence: we are all masculine men. This is the basic energy that drives us from deep inside. It is the energy that determines the way we feel and makes us happy. I believe in men with male energy.

During our life we adapt in response to events and life challenges. We do this to survive as human beings. Regardless of the nature of these events and challenges, the intensity with which we experience them shapes us during our lifetime. This adaptation is a result of a basic fear that is rooted deep inside each and every one of us, namely that we are not good enough as we are, and therefore the people that matter most to us in life won't love us.

This fear is such a strong motivator that we force ourselves to adapt to whatever we feel will retain that love, in order to prove to our source of love that we are worthy. It works for us in the moment, so we stick to the strategy!

It is through this adaptation that we put our authentic selves to sleep. Part of this is the masculine energy inside us. We shift away from the connection to our inner core and leave it behind, as we perceive it as too dangerous and in many cases too painful to remember.

As we grow into adulthood, this adapted masculinity becomes more confused about the role it plays in our life. There are several reasons for this.

Our fathers, mothers, teachers, peers, and the media are very happy to present us with role models of masculinity and, using symbols and archetypes, construct images based on socially accepted rules as anchors for us to grab onto. We unconsciously embrace these ideals and adapt to them.

Following the growth of the strength of women, men were invited to join in household life, and women took on jobs in the workforce. This led to a reversal of roles, and more equality in the relationship. This is often referred to as "new" or "integrated" masculinity, though perhaps "confused" is more appropriate.

People believed this newfound equality in relationships was the solution to many problems, in their personal life as well as in their relationships. But looking around in today's western society, it is clear to me that something else is needed. Most people are still not feeling fulfilled. The question is why not? What else do we need?

The answer is that we need to reawaken those parts of ourselves that are dormant within us and find our own "Personal Masculinity."

Having grown through our personal life experiences to a stage of sharing and equality, men are now ready to clear up the confusion by adding their true core to the mix. This means moving away from society's and parent's role models and discovering who we really are at our core. One of the major elements in this is the reawakening of our own male characteristics.

In rousing the dormant parts of ourselves we will become whole, and once we are whole we will no longer need people or material goods around us to fill the void inside us. We will be complete and from that completeness we will act and behave differently, as we connect from a place of feeling at ease within ourselves.

From this place of completeness, we will create a new type of relationship with the people around us, as we no longer feel dependent. In an intimate relationship where a clearly defined masculine essence is present, a strong polarity is created, a polarity that can be missing in a relationship based on equality.

We will step up and be men again.

Living a
"Not for Granted" Life

by Cindi Wilson

Cindi Wilson is a global business transformation consultant, author, travel addict, and self-proclaimed "Life Passionista," striving to *never* take life for granted! She resides in Luxembourg and can be found at her personal website: www.cindiwilson.com.

After many years in the international corporate world, she stopped, designed a "Mid-life Reinvention" and traveled the world for two years, writing about the experience as well as the personal growth and insights that developed as a result. She is passionate about enjoying life as an adventure, seeing the beauty in every moment, and appreciating the people around us. She now works as a consultant, merging her business experience with her international savvy and "can-do" enthusiasm for her clients.

She is a contributing author to *The Gratitude Book Project: Celebrating 365 Days of Gratitude, 2012 Edition,* and *The Gratitude Book Project: Celebrating Moms & Motherhood.* Look for her future books: *Living a "Not for Granted" Life,* two books on her travels, and several others under way.

As an advocate of motivation and personal development, she has participated in Tony Robbins "Unleash the Power Within" and Fire-walk, Chris Howard's Academy of Wealth and Achievement and

Advanced Presentation Skills training, and several Internet marketing and branding seminars in Europe and the USA.

When not writing or traveling, Cindi is an award-winning Business Transformation Consultant; specialising in quality and customer satisfaction for global corporations. She has previously held positions as Director of Quality and Customer Satisfaction and Vice President of Global Supplier Quality, and lived in the USA, Europe, and Singapore. She also has been a conference speaker, coach, and winner of European Six Sigma awards. Creating turn-around quality performance, capable suppliers, and increased business for clients is a passion. To find out more, see her business website www.cindiwilson.me or her profile on LinkedIn: http://www.linkedin.com/in/cindiwilson.

Another Day in Paradise

I live in a small country and the last remaining Grand Duchy in the world. It is so small; I can be in three other countries in 20 minutes. With smallness comes ease and familiarity. Here the featured news centers on upcoming social events, insignificant events (like stolen garden gnomes), or strange events (like the Duke's dryer catching on fire)—not tragedy. It's an idyllic, nearly fairytale land, dotted with castles on rolling green countryside and encased in old European charm. It's where a multitude of languages are spoken, and contented cows seem to outnumber the residents. Profitable financial institutions abound, and the standard of life is high. Even the cows appear to magically levitate in the air, their legs unseen, shrouded in the haze of the cool white morning mist.

Yes, it's a good life, and the lack of significant economic, social, or cultural problems makes it easy to take it for granted. But sometimes, certain events will bring us back to reality, and shock us into awareness of just how fragile and precious life really is. One of those events recently happened to me. It opened my eyes and I realized that I needed to be more conscious, more appreciative, and more grateful—but mostly to *never* take anything for granted.

Moreover, I realised that I needed to consider applying "not for granted" to every area of my life, and that this was something important enough to share with you.

...But Unlike Any Other

This is not just a story about appreciation and gratitude; it is much more than that. It's about seeing your life with new eyes and developing a sensual acuity that allows you to *really* feel. Then it's about taking the actions required to make your life more amazing than you ever could imagine.

I want to tell you this story to wake you up. I want to "teach you to see" so you can be fully aware. I want you to feel an incredible, passionate life, filled with love, connection, and beauty. I want you to have meaningful relationships, monumental achievements, heartfelt happiness, and the ability to change the world of those around you.

All of this is possible. And a few small changes can yield life-changing results.

If you take this journey with me, I promise you a richer, more fulfilled life in a mere thirty days. Is that a skeptical look I see on your face? Yes, it is possible. But you will need to be honest with yourself, and it will require a little work. The road isn't always easy. Sometimes, it's a little bumpy, and sometimes you have to step out of your comfort zone. However, I have always believed, "All tough journeys result in great destinations." Don't worry … I have the map, and I'm coming with you. So, let's get started…

> *"One's destiny is never a place, but a new way of seeing things."*
> – Henry Miller

The Realisation

My calm paradise had been shocked. In five summer days, there have been four fatal car accidents, and I have been within minutes of two of them. Let me tell you about one of them. I was driving through the woods, the two-lane road shaded by the thick expanse of trees on either side. I was on my way to my outdoor "Forest Fit" fitness class when I saw brilliant blue lights flashing behind me. That was the ambulance. It was followed by two emergency vehicles, a police car, a fire truck, and an automobile club emergency car.

All traffic came to an abrupt standstill, and long lines soon weaved in both directions, waiting for whatever was ahead to clear. I knew in an instant that this was serious, and silently prayed, "Let them be OK," but a solemn heaviness filled the air.

Minutes later, the ambulance raced back, but we still were not moving. Finally, after forty-five minutes, a fireman appeared from the woods and told us all to turn around and go back. One by one, each car made a choreographed U-turn to leave. Whatever was ahead was either impassable or something they didn't want us to see.

Inevitably, I missed my fitness class, and as I turned around, a soft rain started again, misting my windshield. Probably the dampness from the earlier rain on the smooth, shady road was part of the reason for the accident.

For the forty-five minutes I sat in my car, going nowhere, I started to think. I thought of the person or persons involved in that accident…Someone wasn't coming home tonight. Someone's life might be changed forever after this moment, or their life may not exist at all. Someone's loved ones will be getting tragic news, and their lives will be changed forever too.

I wondered if they had a family or were in a family, where they worked, who would miss them, and what contributions they were making to the world with their life—and where they were rushing to on this evening. I wondered who else had been involved, as runners and bicyclists also use this narrow road through the woods, or if there had been passengers.

Then, with a sudden shock, I also realized that, had I left a few minutes earlier, *it could have been me.*

No one knows. No one expects that today might be their last, yet every day, the unknown happens. No one imagines that they might not see their loved ones again. Every day we go about our business, assuming, expecting, *taking for granted* that our lives will go on.

The Costs of Sleepwalking Through Life

Because of that expectation, many of us don't truly live, or love, or appreciate, or enjoy. We simply exist in busy lives, without thought or feeling. Many of us "sleepwalk" through life, focused on "what's next," not "what's now." Not only do we not live in the moment, we often fail to appreciate those who mean the most to us, and even worse, fail to let them know how much they do.

How can we better appreciate the fleeting beauty of life itself? How can we become conscious? What do we need to do to make it meaningful? Whether we have nine or ninety years, do we really know how to love the people in our life and enjoy life while we have it?

Years ago, when I was in university, I read the book *Real Moments*, by Barbara DeAngelis, and later when going through a divorce, I came across *The Precious Present*, by Spencer Johnson. Both of these books had a profound influence on me, and I made a commitment to make a conscious effort to be "conscious."

Yes, I realised happiness was not a destination, but a journey moment-to-moment in my everyday life. I did stop and smell the roses, and I did offer mental thanks for the natural beauty of a sunset. But I hadn't told the people around me how much they meant to me, appreciated the job that provided a good living, or thought much about the place that I lived. I was busy, sometimes too busy to notice, say something, or take action. After all, there was still time, right? I was sure that people *understood* how I felt, so I didn't need to make any special efforts to show or tell them what they already knew. But I was wrong.

I think "taking someone for granted" is the biggest reason for marital breakups—I think it was for mine. In fact, I think it's the biggest reason families aren't closer, don't communicate well, and miss having heartfelt connections.

I also think it's the biggest reason for depression. We simply fail to see, recognise, and acknowledge that what we have—right now— is pretty good. I think it's the reason people are stuck in impassionate lives—existing, but not really living. It is a waste for humanity when they could become so much more.

I think it's the reason people ignore their health. Believing they'll live forever, they fail to exercise and eat without limitation.

We need to *wake up*! It's time to take the beauty and fragility of life seriously, to take stock of your life, to realise that the familiar is extraordinary, and most importantly, to never take anything for granted.

> *"To my mind, the greatest reward and luxury of travel is to be able to experience everyday things as if for the first time, to be in a position in which almost nothing is so familiar it is taken for granted."*
> —Bill Bryson

Waking Up—Becoming Aware and Learning to See

Life is often repetitive. Daily schedules become routine. With every day that goes by we get accustomed to "the sameness" and gradually don't even see our surroundings, which simply become "white noise" that we tune out. We do this with our house, our workplace, and unfortunately, even the people we live with.

We even drive on "autopilot." How many times have you driven to work along the same route, had your mind on other things, and arrived only to realise you hadn't noticed anything along the way? Scary, isn't it? Yet we do it all the time.

Let's get out of this complacency! It's time to retrain yourself "to see" again. One of the exercises I use is "Learning to See." To do this, you will look at your familiar surroundings with new eyes. You will approach as if you have never been there before and are a stranger seeing it for the first time.

Let's take an example. I applied this technique to "seeing" my own house as if for the first time. I pretended to put myself in the shoes of a new neighbor coming to introduce themselves. As I, the stranger, approach my house, this is what I observe:

First, I like the way it is positioned on a hill with a forest behind. It seems serene. But as I pass my mailbox, I notice that the house number is very faded, and wonder how the postman and visitors find me. Walking up the steps, I observe the entryway is nicely framed by two planters, but the brown-tinged shrubs inside them look like they need some water, and there is some peeling paint on the lamp post.

As I enter the foyer, I like the dramatic sweep of the staircase and the Mediterranean paintings, but notice that there are five pairs of shoes, two suitcases, three briefcases, two jackets, and a small library worth of books stacked just off to the side. (I later sign up for a "Declutter Your House" class after this exercise.)

The kitchen, although functional and tidy, has a large stack of mail on the countertop. Walking into the adjoining living room, I notice that the colors are muted, I see a large armchair and footrest in floral tapestry fabric, chiffon white sheers blow in the breeze, and there are lots of mirrors, candles and flowers. A Venetian lamp with pink magnolia globes highlights the delicate carving on a wooden, four-panel divider. While I like this décor, I notice that it is very feminine, and I wonder what male visitors think when they visit.

I could go on to every room, but I think you get the idea. Every day I walked into this house, but rarely had I been aware of what it really looked like. You can learn a lot by looking again at the familiar with "new eyes," "fresh eyes," or "eyes wide open."

Exercise: Now it's your turn. Try it yourself. Enter your house from the street, as if you were seeing it for the first time. Imagine yourself as someone else. Now—what do you see? What do you like? What don't you like? What would be your first impression? What conclusions would you draw about yourself based on what you see? What would you want to change? Write down your observations. What actions will you take as a result of these observations? Where else would you like to do this exercise? Perhaps at your business or office? What would your clients think?

Finished? Excellent! You are doing great. You have "learned to see." Isn't it amazing what is suddenly visible when you are aware, when you really open your eyes—when you don't take things for granted?

> *"We live in a wonderful world that is full of beauty, charm, and adventure.*
> *There is no end to the adventures we can have if we seek them with our eyes open."*
> —Jawaharial Nehru

Experiencing What You Feel

Now you can see, but you also need to feel. Wherever you are right now, I want you to become aware. Let's get started:

1. **Where are you?** Maybe you are in an armchair in your living room, in bed, propped up on pillows, outdoors on a porch swing, by the ocean in a hammock, in a desk chair in front of your computer, sitting on a train listening on mp3, in a cabin or lying on a rug in front of a fire.

2. **Wherever you are, what does your chair or support feel like?** How soft or hard is the surface that is supporting you? Are your feet up? Is the material soft? What are the colors?

3. **What is the temperature?** Is it warm or cool? Are you indoors or outdoors? Is there a breeze? Can you hear the birds? Or someone's lawn mower? Or music? Is it day

or night? What are you wearing? How do your clothes feel on your body?

4. **Is someone with you?** Are family members, friends, or a significant other in the room? What are they doing? Is a dog sitting at your feet or a cat stretched out on the couch, or some fish swimming in a fishbowl? What is the feeling in the room between you and these others?

5. **How do you feel?** Are you rested or tired? Are you focused or distracted? Are you comfortable, hungry, thirsty, relaxed, or content? Or are you thinking of other things at the same time as you are trying to be aware of your surroundings?

Just for a moment, block out the outside world, and focus only on you and this moment. Just feel.

Exercise: Now write down where you are, what you feel, and your answers to some of the questions above.

Do you have a greater sense of what is around you and your existence? Does your life feel richer than simply "reading a book" right now?

It feels good, doesn't it? It's expansive, this awareness, and a critical step to not taking things for granted.

Getting in Touch with the State of "For Granted"

Now that you feel, let's get in touch with feelings and reactions to being "taken for granted." Have you ever been taken for granted? Sure, we probably all have at some time…perhaps by our parents, our spouse, our friends, or our boss. Let's look at some questions and some feelings:

1. **What is the state of "For Granted?"**
   An unconscious state, going through the motions without thought, automated lives, engaging in numbing mindless activities …

- Always expecting something to be there
- Not caring, not feeling fortunate
- Comfortable, predictable, boring
- Feeling "entitled," lack of appreciation
- Negative or neutral

Just reading these words puts you in a depressed state!

2. **How do you feel when you are being "taken for granted?"** Think for a moment of a situation when you felt this way, and how it made you feel. Can you describe those feelings? You might say:
   - Not good enough, inferior, not special, I don't matter
   - Empty, sad, negative
   - Unloved
   - Unappreciated, unrecognised for your efforts
   - Predictable, routine, mundane
   - Complacent

It doesn't feel very good, does it?

3. **What is your reaction when you are being taken for granted?** Do you:
   - Stop caring
   - Stop trying to please
   - Stop working
   - Get angry
   - Try to get someone's attention in unusual ways
   - Get depressed, unhappy
   - Lose confidence
   - Eat, drink, or take some "numbing" medication or drug to alleviate the emotional pain
   - Leave
   - Find someone else who pays attention and makes you feel good

No wonder relationships fail when you take someone for granted.

4. **How do you feel when you realize you have taken someone for granted?**
    - Guilty
    - Regretful
    - Sad

    Or is it already too late, and you feel loss…or realise you let something that was once special slip away?

5. **How do you feel when you are noticed and appreciated?**
    - Loved
    - Confident
    - Valued, needed
    - Thankful
    - Excited
    - Anticipation to see them
    - Passion, happiness
    - Positive that someone believes in you

    Basically, you feel good about yourself!

6. **How do you react when you are appreciated and not "taken for granted?"**
    - Giving, caring
    - Loving, passionate
    - Positive
    - Helpful
    - Sharing
    - Hardworking
    - Reciprocating
    - Responsible, loyal
    - Doing something special or above and beyond expectations

    It looks like it's a foundation to all good relationships.

7. **Great! Now you know how it feels…But how can you specifically make others feel "not for granted" in your life? Here are some actions you can employ:**
   - Tell them you love them
   - Tell them the things you love about them
   - Spend time together
   - Ask how you can help…or help without asking
   - Displays of affection
   - Memories / reminiscing
   - Random acts of kindness
   - Special favors
   - Say "Thank you"
   - Compliment them
   - Apologise
   - Do something that makes them happy
   - Send emails of information they can use
   - Surprise notes
   - Respect and courtesy
   - Anticipate their needs
   - Pick up on clues they have dropped
   - Do "Little things"
   - Reciprocate
   - Date nights

Top Twelve Areas to Focus Your "Not for Granted" Life

Now let's look at twelve key areas of your life where you can apply it. We will step through each one with tips on how to make each area significant in your life:

1. Yourself

Some people will do anything for others, but neglect their own spirit. To truly be able to give of yourself to others, you have to love yourself first.

There is no one else like you. Take a moment and think about what makes you special. Acknowledge and celebrate what is uniquely you.

Exercise: Make a list of thirty things you love about yourself. If you have been neglecting yourself, you may have a slow start. Step outside of yourself and see your talents, what you do for others, how others see you, what you do better than other people, and special qualities that are characteristically you.

2.   Partner, Spouse, or Significant Other

You fell in love for a reason. Do you remember why? What was it you loved about them? Or was it how they made you feel about you?

If you forget why, or take them for granted, a long-term relationship can easily fall into a boring and predictable pattern. Criticism causes a relationship to deteriorate, so try and remember the magic that brought you together. See them again for the first time.

Exercise: Make a list of thirty things you love (or loved) about your partner. Create a "Valentine" that lives beyond Valentine's Day. Start your list of "Why I love you" and keep adding to it all year long.

Reinvigorate and reinforce your love and connection. Think about what matters to them. Do little things to let them know you still care and think about them, things that show that they are still special to you and are the most important person in your life. It's also just as important to acknowledge and appreciate all the little things that they do for you.

Be inspired by the Tom Robbins quote: *"We waste time looking for the perfect lover, instead of creating the perfect love."* You can make your relationship your perfect love.

3.   Family—Parents, Siblings, Children

Our parents were the most significant people in our lives as we grew up. Not everyone had a great relationship, but for most they provided food, shelter, values, transportation, money, time, and teaching. They were probably the easiest people to take for granted. Breakfast appeared, laundry was done, and we were taken to school. It was simply expected. Often we never realized what they gave up to bring us into the world or support us until we were independent.

As our parents age, we finally begin to understand their efforts and the great impact they had on us. When we lose them we are suddenly confronted with the realisation that life isn't forever, and we lose a link to our history. Sometimes this is without warning. I had a friend whose mother was tragically run over one day in a supermarket parking lot, when someone reversed their vehicle and didn't see her, instantly killing her. Another learned of the sudden loss of her mother while she was on holiday in Iceland, hearing by phone that her depressed mother pulled the trigger in the garden, fatally shooting herself. I lost a father who was only in his sixties, due to a debilitating disease. One friend's father died, and now my friend fears losing her mother with each passing year, as one day, at ninety it will be inevitable.

If you have been waiting to say "I love you" to these important people, wait no more. Think about what they gave to you and what they mean in your life right now.

Siblings share our history. Only they can truly understand our home life. They were confidants, playmates, and competitors vying for parents' time and attention. They know your story, and you have a connection like no other. Do you remember special moments you shared? Remind them that they hold a special place in your life.

Children are a source of wonder, inspiration, imitation, innovation, and they are miniature models of ourselves. We see the world with new eyes when we see it through the eyes of a child. When we pay attention to a child, their self-esteem grows. Taking a child for granted is inflicting a slow death to their spirit. Children need to know daily that they are loved. Besides telling them, how else can you show them that they are appreciated and supported by you? How can you make sure you show your children that each one is special, unique, and loved? No child is interchangeable or replaceable. What joy do they bring into your life? If you don't have children of your own, perhaps there are other children in your life that are equally important to you.

Grandparents and extended relatives add spice to our lives, helping define the band of people we call "family" and shaping our identity. Aunts, uncles, cousins, nieces, and nephews all contribute to our family life, so don't just meet at weddings and funerals. How have they inspired you, touched you, or helped you? Don't forget to let them know.

Who are the key family members in your life, and how have they impacted you? What do you love and appreciate about them? Remember to tell your family you care about them. Often, one of the deepest regrets people have is never having said "I love you" to a family member before they die.

4. Pets

Nothing provides unconditional love like a dog. Pets can be the children you never had, the playmate for children, or the companion that keeps you from feeling lonely. They can be a source of fun, laughter, and joy. If you have a pet, think about what make makes it special and what it adds to your life.

5. Friends and Colleagues

Your friends are anchors who ground you when needed or let you sail away when it's time to fly. They support you, challenge you, cry with you, laugh with you, cheer for you, and lend a helping hand. In our mobile society, friends move in and out of our life as we or they move, change jobs, or switch schools. But for all the changes, we never forget how they touched our heart.

Think of the friends who were with you throughout various stages of your life. Who were your significant childhood friends, friends in high school, and in university? Who pulled pranks, stood up for you, cajoled you when you were down, or helped you with your homework? Who did you confide in about boyfriends or girlfriends, and who was with you when you married? Who shared rides, emergencies, conversation over coffee, or barbeques in all the places you've lived? Think of the moments when things may have turned out differently had they not been there.

Colleagues are friends at work. Who helped lighten your workload, listened to your presentation, gave you feedback on your dilemmas, or coached you to ask for a raise?

Don't lose touch with the friends who were always there for you. Who are they? What value did they give you? Find them, reconnect, laugh over the old memories and start some new ones. Enhance your relationship with new friends currently in your life as well.

6. Teachers and Mentors

Someone had a major influence on you. Maybe they inspired you or were a role model. Maybe they taught you to learn or got you interested in a specific topic. Maybe that became your profession. Maybe they had an impact on the direction you took in life, where you live, your ability to create wealth, or your capacity to love. Maybe they took you under their wing and mentored you, to help you avoid problems, and succeed.

Who were they? What impact did they have on your life? What did you do differently because of them? Have you ever told them the meaning they provided in your life? Telling them would add a true sense of meaning to their life's work.

7. Where You Live

Where do you live? Is it in a small town, a big town, in the city, in the country, near mountains, near a lake or ocean, on what continent, and what country? Is this your home country or a new country you call home? What is your house like? What do you like about it? Do you enjoy your neighbors? What is the weather like? What events, festivals, activities, clubs, culture, classes, sports and social engagements does it offer you? How do you give back to your community?

8. Where You Work

Are you fortunate to have a job, career, or business that provides a steady income and benefits? Are there growth and learning opportunities? Do you travel and experience new places? Does your office have good camaraderie and team spirit? Do you have a title, office, car, phone, or assistant? Is your job a source of responsibility, pride, and self-esteem? What if you lost it?

9. People Who Serve You

Think also of those who perform some service for you. How do you greet them? Do you acknowledge them? Do you look them in the eye and smile? Do you thank them? Yes, maybe it is their job, but they have the same need for connection and significance that you do. Their jobs are no less meaningful. Their jobs help the quality of your life.

You have daily encounters with the fruit stacker at the grocery store, the cashier, the gas station attendant, the office cleaner, the person taking your food order, the toilet attendant, the drycleaner, and many others. They are not invisible. Who are they in your life? Next time, really see them, acknowledge them, and thank them. Not only will you have helped them have a good day, their pride will increase, and you will probably receive better service as a result.

10. Your Health

Our health is one of the biggest things we take for granted—until we don't have it anymore. There is a joke that goes, "If I knew I would live this long, I would have taken better care of myself." Think of all the functions your body performs of which you aren't even conscious. What condition are you in? What do you like about your body and senses? What activities do you enjoy that your body allows you to do? What should you be doing to maintain or improve your health?

11. Your Spirituality

Perhaps you believe in a God, a creator, higher being, divine source, or entity of any other name that provides you comfort and inspiration. Does this entity, your church, or religion fill a need in your life?

12. The Things You Love

Think of all the things you love to do or all those things you cherish that you own. Do they satisfy a need or give you joy? What hobbies, activities, and sports do you enjoy? What possessions are you proud of or grateful for? What would be the quality of your life without them?

Do you play? Remember when you were a child and everything was a wonder and anytime could be playtime? Do you take any time out of your day for fun? Smell the roses, walk in the rain, play catch, jump in a pile of leaves, make snow angels, or simply lie back on the ground and look up at the shapes of the clouds. Be spontaneous. Don't forget to nourish the child still within you.

"We can only be said to be alive in those moments
when our hearts are conscious of our treasures."
—Thornton Wilder

Now that you have considered all of these areas of your life, does it seem richer? If you stop and think for a moment…aware of all you have, seeing what is around you, really feeling and being in touch with your surroundings…does it add a whole new dimension to your life? What—and who—have you been taking for granted? How do you want to change that? How quickly do you want to start?

Living the "Not for Granted" Life

You've looked at all the people, places, and things you love in your life. Hopefully, it has been a positive reminder of how you got to be you, everything you have, and how fortunate you really are in this moment.

I'm sure you've come to some realizations, including:

- Who matters most in your life.
- What is really important to you.
- What you might have been denying yourself.
- Who or what makes you happy.
- Who you need to connect with or appreciate.
- Who you need to tell you love them.

It has also probably been a reminder of what is no longer in your life, people you miss, or opportunities not taken to connect. Now that you know, don't just set this book down and walk away. You've taken the first critical step to enhancing your life. Now that you know it, you've got to show it. It's time to set a plan for your next steps and follow through.

Remember…I promised you a richer, more fulfilled life in thirty days. Thirty days—that's all it takes. But if you want to achieve it, you need to take action—*now*. Put the love back into your life and put the *life* back into your life.

Setting Your Action Plan for the Next Thirty Days

How can you change your life in thirty days? Easy! You have a mission for the next four weeks. In the twelve areas I have highlighted, you will focus on three per week. That means you will address these areas each week:

Week 1:   Yourself;
Partner, Spouse, or Significant Other;
Family—Parents, Siblings, Children

Week 2:   Pets;
Friends and Colleagues;
Teachers and Mentors

Week 3:   Where You Live;
Where You Work;
People Who Serve You

Week 4:   Your Health;
Your Spirituality;
The Things You Love

The first week is quite significant and may require the most effort, because it deals with people closest to you. It may also yield the greatest impact, as your relationships change and grow, carrying results forward into the following weeks. Continue to look at the three new areas each week and make contact, acknowledge, or appreciate.

By the end of the fourth week, you will have an immeasurable difference in your life. You will have also created a ripple effect of goodwill even greater than yourself. The total benefit of your actions you may never know, but you will have touched both yourself and humanity.

You *can* have an incredible, passionate life, filled with love, connection, and beauty. You *can* have meaningful relationships, monumental achievements, heartfelt happiness, and the ability to change the world of those around you. All of it *is* possible, and a few small changes *can* yield life-changing results.

It isn't that difficult, but it can mean the world to you and those around you. It's up to you to make that difference.

> Step up!
> You know what to do.
> Choose not to simply live life, but to live with passion.
> Take action now and truly live a "not for granted" life.

> *"Twenty years from now you will be more disappointed by the things you didn't do than by the ones you did do. So throw off the bowlines, sail away from the safe harbour. Catch the trade winds in your sails.*
> *Explore. Dream. Discover"*
> —Mark Twain

Getting More "Grateful" in Your Life to Stop "For Granted"

You are now aware that taking things "for granted" stops you from living a fulfilling life and achieving goals. It supports limiting beliefs, complacency, and lack of action and acceptance of the status quo. Here are some more things you can do:

1. Every morning when you wake up, take a few minutes to think of all the things you are grateful for in your life. Do the same when you go to bed at night. Keeping a notebook for this can be particularly rewarding.
2. Tell your loved ones how special they are.
3. Make a "bucket list" of all the things you want to do or experience in your lifetime - and don't wait until retirement to do it.
4. If you have big dreams, take daily steps toward making them a reality. There will never be a perfect time, so don't wait for conditions to be right. You have today. Make it happen. Do it now.

5. Don't wait! Don't wait to live or to celebrate. Don't wait for a special occasion for the good wine or the good china—*life* is a special occasion.

No one's life is perfect. Maybe there are challenges in your daily life and perhaps you experienced a difficult past, but your past is not your destiny. The nice thing about life is that it teaches us many lessons:

1. Don't miss the joy in your life because you still exist in the past. You can't undo your past, but you can choose your present.
2. Measure your happiness by what you *do* have, not by what's missing in your life.
3. The more you appreciate, the more you attract positive energy, which will bring even more into your life to appreciate. Like attracts like. Being grateful opens the door to abundance.

"Life's not about waiting for the storms to pass…
It's about learning to dance in the rain."
—Vivian Greene

Live Life *LARGE*

I have one last tip to help you live a "not for granted" life. You simply need to live life LARGE!

By LARGE, I mean:

L   Living in the moment
A   Awareness and appreciation
R   Recognising what's important
G   Gratitude
E   Expression

If you remember this model, you'll never live a "for granted" life.

Here's to your happiness!

"I'm listening...
Flowers in the garden,
Laughter in the hall,
Children in the park,
I will not take these things for granted
...Anymore."
—Toad the Wet Sprocket

Relationships Are the Foundation of Any Business

by Ruth Thirtle

After fifteen years of hospitality management and recruitment experience, Ruth Thirtle established her own business, Your Abundance Now, and she is now known as The Business Results Catalyst. Ruth helps business owners with "Inspiring Profitable Conversations" and to use relationship marketing strategies to boost their business relationships and profits. She has worked with the world's largest business referral organisations, including BNI and 4Networking.

Ruth blogs regularly for the Business Blogging Network, Women's Network Australia, and her own blog, BusinessNetworker. In addition she is an NLP certified Master Coach and on the advisory board for the Professional Coaches Network. She is an in-demand speaker at business and networking events and has contributed to a number of business books, including *The Power of 100, Mind Your Own Business and SocMed: Social Media for Business.*

Through her virtual business bootcamp, "ADVANCE Your Business," she helps people to learn and implement the five keys to business success through strong business relationships.

In the 1950s and 1960s, scientist Harry Harlow conducted a series of experiments with infant Rhesus monkeys. During the experiments they withdrew contact and affection (relationship) from a group of the monkeys. In a nutshell, Harlow discovered that the monkeys who were deprived of a relationship with their mother in the early stages of development did not fare so well in physical and social ways as the group that were with the mother.

Prior to these experiments, it was assumed that the bond between mother and infant was strong because of meeting primal needs such as hunger, thirst, and pain-relief. These experiments countered that and showed that the needs of relationship went beyond that. In fact, it was the relating itself that was the basis for thriving in life.

I believe that business is exactly the same: it is the relationships that form the basis for the thriving, successful business.

When I first started my coaching and training business, I was focusing on mindset and marketing strategy. I do still believe that those two things are crucial for business success; however, I am also a firm believer that the relationships that you have in business are the foundations of your business. Strong relationships can assist you in building an impressive, extravagant business. Weak relationships will make it very difficult to sustain any meaningful business results for very long.

If we begin from the standpoint that people want to help people (not always true but a good assumption to begin with for your own success and sanity), then we need to help people to help us. We need to help them to have conversations about us and encourage them to be in relationship with us.

This chapter will predominantly focus on the relationship between the business owner or employee and the prospects or customers. However, as you read I would encourage you to also consider the other relationships involved in running a business such as:

Employers with employees
Businesses with suppliers
Referral partners with prospects
Strategic alliance partners with customers

The list really could go on and on.

In this chapter I will explore five practical strategies for developing and nurturing relationships that have the potential to be long-lasting, fun, and potentially lucrative. They certainly represent the way that I do business.

The strategies are:

1) Open a relationship—don't close a sale
2) Give people something to talk about
3) Enjoy and join the conversation
4) Don't assume that people know anything
5) Be authentic and embrace uniqueness

My hope is that you will assess the way you relate to people in the context of your business—not to be upset with yourself, just to be aware and make any adjustments you might need to make.

Open a Relationship—Don't Close a Sale

Personally, I think that "closing a sale" is one of the most unfortunate terms in the English language.

There are many dictionary definitions for the word "close." Here is just a selection:

To stop the operations of permanently or temporarily: *closed down the factory.*

To make unavailable for use: *closed the area to development; closed the database to further changes.*

To bring to an end; terminate: *close a letter; close a bank account.*

To bring together all the elements or parts of: *Management closed ranks and ostracized the troublemaker.*

Why on earth would we want to think about doing business with someone in these kinds of terms?

From a logical point of view, it is generally known to cost ten times more to acquire a new customer than it does to retain, and sell more to, an existing customer. Therefore considering the first time someone buys from you as opening a relationship rather than closing a sale seems logical. From the point of view of ease and pleasure in doing business, thinking in these terms seems to be far more rewarding also.

There are a number of reasons why thinking in terms of opening a relationship rather than closing a sale will be beneficial for the long-term growth and development of your business. Here are my top three.

1) **Market Research.** Your existing customers are a great source of market research for you. When you open a relationship with customers, they will give you feedback on products that they have already bought from you and also let you know what other product they would be interested in receiving from you in future.

What this means for you is that your product creation (or import or retail range) can cost a lot less, be more focused, and far more effective.

Let's say you are a personal trainer. You sell a particular training package to a hundred people. As you stay in contact with them and build the relationship, you start to discuss their problems, their challenges, and their dreams.

You then take the time to ask them whether they would rather have:

a) an audio of affirmations and motivational reasons to achieve their dreams
b) a DVD of exercises
c) a book of healthy recipes as a complement to their current training package

Based on their answers, you create the product: you already have people who have told you they want it and trust you enough to do business with you.

Wouldn't that be easier than "closing a new sale on a new product?"

2) **Constant Improvement**. When you think about closing a sale, there is an end and finality to the transaction.

What a wasted opportunity! Business is competitive and constantly evolving, so there is a need for continual improvement—if you aren't interested in that, you probably shouldn't be in business.

When the exchange of money is another step in a relationship, there is much more opportunity to assess your performance and see how you can improve. This can be as simple as a follow-up questionnaire or a regular card, email, or phone call.

It is important to encourage people to be comfortable giving you honest feedback. Think about personal relationships: are you more likely to give the honest (and maybe difficult) answers to your close friends or mere acquaintances?

The closer the relationship = the more honest feedback = more opportunities to improve.

3) **Referrals**. Someone referred to your business by someone they already have a relationship with and trust is more likely to do business with you than someone who has no personal recommendation.

Being the business that opens a relationship rather than closes a sale opens you up to receiving more referrals.

When you have used the initial sale as a relationship builder, you will take the opportunities to be top of mind. That way, when someone says to them, "Do you know a good…?" you will be the obvious choice.

Let me share with you a seven-step process to building relationships rather than closing sales. I use the process in my own business and work with clients to implement the same.

Step 1. **Give away completely free information.** In an online business, this can be through blog posts or social media updates. In an offline business, this is still a strategy to use. Think about supermarkets giving away recipe cards, store assistants in clothing stores helping to choose the right fit and outfit combinations, and cinemas giving movie reviews in the same place you can find session times and make film selections.

Step 2. **Exchange information or opportunities for personal details.** In the online world, this is offering an "ethical bribe"—exchanging your information product for their email address. In the offline world, this still happens in the form of monthly business card draws, competitions, loyalty cards, and feedback forms.

Step 3. **People buy from you.** (I do have to say that I like this bit!) People see the value in what you have to offer and decide to purchase.

Step 4. **You keep in touch with the people whose details you have collected.** You add value to their world, life, and business. They like what you have to say, so you stay top of mind.

(NB: Steps 3 and 4 are interchangeable)

Step 5. **You get feedback from, make improvements for. and do research with** your existing clients—those people who have already liked and trusted you enough to buy something from you.

Step 6. **People refer other clients to you.** Because of the relationship they already have with you and the value that you offer, why wouldn't they tell others?

Step 7. **People Buy More.** You continue to relate to people, listen to what they have to say, and stay top of mind. Therefore, when you have new products or offers, they are likely to buy things that are relevant to them.

I do have to say that this method of doing business appeals to me much more than closing each individual sale one at a time and then moving on to market for the next client.

Chances are that if you have bought a programme or product online, you will recognise this process. You will be emailed regularly by the person from whom you made your purchase; as you buy, they will give you the option to refer friends or share on social media (or both); and they will offer you additional products of their own or from joint venture partners—some you will buy and some you won't.

As long as they continue to relate to you, provide valuable information, and don't give the impression that they are just about "closing sales," you will probably stay in their community and their world, and you may well buy from them again.

The sale begins when the customer says yes.
—Harvey MacKay

Give People Something to Talk About

I'm sure that it won't surprise you to know that there are conversations happening all over the place about a wide range of subjects. Can you even think about how many conversations you have had so far this week, or even just today?

The best way to build relationships and then build your business is to have conversations happening about you and your business. In order for people to have conversations about you, you need to give them something to talk about.

Again, consider your own personal friendships. When one of your friends is doing good things, everyone talks about them, whether they are there or not. I live in Australia, and when I go back to the UK for a visit, I spend time with friend and families.

When I was at University, there were six of us that spent a year away in the same town in Germany. I will not always catch up with all of them but generally with one or two of that group of people. Some of our time is always spent catching up on what the other members of the group are doing. Depending on what they are doing, some of those conversations are short and some are much longer— and some are more interesting than others. I hope that the conversations they have about me when I'm not there are long and interesting.

With your business and your business relationships, you want people to talk about you in this way as well. You want them to be sharing your business message, the results of your product and service, as well as what you have been doing (and hopefully having the longer, not the shorter conversations).

Let's consider some of the ways that the bigger brands have been built this way, so you may adopt some ideas of what you can do. I am a firm believer that if big business uses a strategy and uses it well yet it does not take a big business budget to do it then everyone can also benefit.

Generate Free Publicity. Having your product or service featured in the media is a great way to get people talking about it. Consistently share the newsworthy parts of what you are doing with the media. This is not about making announcements or specifically "selling" any product. This is about awareness of who you are and what you do and giving people something to talk about.

As an example of this, look at Richard Branson and the Virgin group of companies. I'm sure we could all name our favourite publicity moment generated by Mr. Branson—I personally still have the vision of a certain wedding dress!

Contribute to Charity. This actually fits in with the previous point, as charitable contributions can be leveraged to generate publicity. Now I am a strong believer in charitable contribution, and I was even before I had a business. The contribution came first and will always feature prominently for me—it is not something I have just started in order to benefit my business. However, it is also a subject for people to talk about.

Think about the Bill and Melinda Gates Foundation. Through social media, traditional media, networking events, at parties and over dinner tables, the bold promise of the Foundation has started conversations all over the world.

Be Different. People will talk about something that is different. If you are the same as everyone else, doing the same things in the same way, there is no incentive for people to have conversations about you. If you are doing things in a different way or talking about different issues, then people will remember—and when they remember, they will talk.

Car manufacturers are very good at this. When they launch a new product, they will focus on the things that make them unique or different. Constantly innovating, constantly evolving, constantly doing something different—and telling us about it so we can have conversations about them.

So are you ready to be the topic of conversation at the pub on a Friday afternoon? Or on a social media page? Or at a networking event? And for all of the right reasons?

If you are, here are the steps I would be taking (and have done) to make it happen.

1. **Increase your circle of influence**—and be strategic about it. In order to have people talking about you, you must be talking to more people. And when you talk to more people, and strategically consider the people that you talk to, you are moving towards inspiring profitable conversations.

2. **Go to places where your target clients are likely to be.** This could be business events, training courses, expos or even school football games or the gym. Start to get known by the people that you want to have conversations about you. Be there to join in conversations, and eventually they can be carried on without you.

3. **Have a call to action that is a no-brainer.** Offer something of great conversational value as the "ethical bribe" we spoke of earlier—and put it on your business cards!

4. **Have great conversation-starting questions prepared for when you meet new people.** Conversations about the weather, sport, or politics may or may not be fun for you, and may help you initially to build relationships. However, these are not the conversations that people will continue months, weeks, days, or even hours later.

There are two great places to go to see what subjects' people are having conversations about. You can then do something different to inspire great conversations. Those places are Facebook and Google.

Search and see blog posts and forums and then see on Facebook where people are interacting.

Then ask yourself how you can inspire similar (not the same—remember, be different!) conversations and interactions.

> *"Conversation about the weather is the last refuge of the unimaginative."*
> —Oscar Wilde

Enjoy and Join the Conversation

So once you have inspired the conversation, you then need to do as Twitter says and "Join the Conversation." This is a really fun way to build a business, so please feel free to enjoy the process!

You start the relationship by giving people the opportunity to talk about you, and you build the relationship by joining in with the conversations that people are having.

I remember the first time that one of my mentors responded to me personally on Facebook, I was very impressed and excited. And in turn, I know that there were people on my list that have received a personal email or comment on social media from me, and it has excited them—and inspired them to keep saying good things about me.

There are a few things to remember when you join the conversation:

> **Your positioning is important.** When people are talking about your product and service, they are positioning you as someone who knows what they are talking about. So when you join the conversation, continue to consider this positioning—you are the expert, you know what you are doing, and you possess useful information.
>
> **Add value to the conversation.** My mum taught me that if I didn't have anything nice to say, I shouldn't say anything. That was very good advice! I would go a step further and say that if you don't have something constructive or valuable to say, then don't say it. Don't just be in the conversation for conversation's sake or for the

sake of selling something! Take the time to answer someone's question, pay them ′ a compliment, or congratulate them on the things they are saying and doing.

Make it personal. When you have a conversation with a friend, you talk to them. It doesn't seem as though you are talking to the whole world through them. Listen to what people are saying and respond to that—don't use the fact that people are having a conversation about you to tell them what you wanted to say in the first place, whether it is appropriate or not.

Be Strategic, Add Value, and Remember That Is All about Building Relationships

Before you join in any conversation, ask yourself these five questions; then you will be both strategic and appropriate—a winning combination!

1) **What is my intention for joining this conversation?** People respond to your intent better and quicker than what you say or do. This means that if your intent is right, you can make all the mistakes in the world and you'll be forgiven, even gain empathy. But if your intentions are not pure, it won't matter how good your conversation skills are, people will go the other way.

2) **Do I have valuable and useful information to add here?** Don't just join in a conversation for the sake of it. It is really enjoyable to join a conversation, either online or in person, and have something great to share or to add. Be generous with your information and your knowledge, and have fun using that to build some great relationships.

3) **Can I further my relationship with these people by paying a compliment here?** What better way to start a conversation than by saying something nice to someone? Now this is not paying a compliment simply for what you can get in return—this is about genuinely

edifying the people around you, being grateful for them, and building rapport.

4) **What is the most personal thing I can say that will make a difference?** When you join a conversation, coming from a place of service rather than sales is a great foundation. When you come from that place, you will reach out to people personally and be constantly considering how you can most make a difference for them.

5) **What can I hint that I do that will make a difference here long term?** (That's the really strategic bit!) I truly believe that business karma means that being the right person with the right intent pays huge dividends—however those dividends may not be immediately financial.

And at the end of the day, if we want to continue being in business we need to make money. So letting people know what you do and that you have products or services that can help them or others is important. So do drop hints and let people know that they can invest in themselves and in you and work further with you.

I used to love watching the shows like Jonathan Ross and Parkinson where one person was interviewed, then they would bring in the next guest, and then a third could join in, and then the next one, etc. At the time, before I was in business, I just found it entertaining the way that the interviews were enhanced by additional involvement. Now I look at it and think that not only were the interviews enhanced but that these interviews were of great benefit to the relationships between the interviewees. By joining in the interview (conversation) and adding value, what sort of strategic relationships could begin to develop? I would love to know…

A good conversationalist is not one who remembers what was said, but says what someone wants to remember.
—John Mason Brown

Don't Assume That People Know Anything

You may have heard the saying that to "assume" is to make an "ass" of "u" and "me." Well, I am here to tell you that it is absolutely true! Relationships in business, as in many other areas of life, are best built on trust and mutual respect. Assumptions really can destroy a relationship right from the outset.

Have you ever spoken to someone who is much more academically or technically smart than you—and likes to make sure that you know it? How did that make you feel?

In the same vein, have you ever had a conversation with someone who assumes that you know nothing? Or that you know much less than you actually do? Just as annoying, isn't it?

It is important with our businesses that we meet people where they stand and relate to them there. In their book *Made to Stick, Chip* and Dan Heath tell us:

"There is value in sequencing information—not dumping a stack of information on someone at once but dropping a clue, then another clue, then another. This method of communication resembles flirting more than lecturing."

So my question is this: Does flirting or lecturing most develop and nurture a relationship?

Here are some things to consider when you are building business relationships either one-to-one or one to many, while also avoiding assumptions:

>**Tastes like chicken.** When describing a meat they have not yet tried, someone will often say that it tastes like chicken...but when we are having conversations this is a great way to avoid technical jargon. Meet people where they currently stand with something that you both know and understand, then take them where you want them to go.
>
>**Clarify abbreviations.** You might think that everyone in the world knows the meaning of EFT, NLP or CRM, but not everyone does. For your market, you may not need to go into huge detail, but mentioning what the initials stand for is a worthwhile move (Emotional Freedom Technique, Neuro-

Linguistic Programming, and Customer Relationship Management in my examples).

Tell stories. Stories are a great part of sharing a message and building relationships. One of the reasons that they are so effective is that you can share a message on multiple levels and explain information in a way that involves everyone. If you are not sure, make an explanation—and be creative in order to keep your audience engaged.

The art is in developing the skills to do this in a "one to many" situation as well as one-to-one.

When you are conversing with someone individually it is easy to see how you are relating to them and whether you are making assumptions—if you are aware and looking for it! When relating to many through video or social media, presenting to a group, or writing website copy, there are a few things you need to do differently.

Here are five mistakes that people make that I would encourage you to avoid:

Mistake # 1. When people don't have a clear enough idea of who they are trying to relate to and do business with, it is very difficult to converse, as it really is impossible to be all things to all people. When you are starting or joining a conversation with many people, a person that would be a great client for you should feel that you are talking only to them even if you know they are one of a thousand.

Mistake # 2. When people don't have a clear personal brand, it is very difficult for them to communicate and relate to people with authenticity and congruence. When your personal brand is truly you and the conversations come from that place, you will avoid rants or comments that do not serve you.

Mistake # 3. SPAM! A single word and that's it. Having a conversation that is just buy from me, buy my stuff: look at my leaflet or web page is SPAM and not beneficial to long-term relationships. Instead, share your knowledge and information, let people know how they will benefit from investing in you, and then give them the opportunity to make a choice. Even when writing a specific sales letter, you should consider that the best converting sales pages are as much about information as they are about sales.

Mistake # 4. A lack of clarity around the problem that someone solves and the solution that they are offering is a huge mistake. I go to a lot of networking events and have lost count of the number of people who have sat down after giving their elevator pitch—and I still have no idea what it is they actually do.

Mistake # 5. People being overly aggressive in their assumption that everyone needs—and therefore wants—their product or service can lead to fewer sales rather than more. There is a fine line between identifying the problems that you are able to help people solve and offending people so they do not want to do business with you.

I will give you an example of mistake number five, as it is quite a balancing act!

A personal trainer is speaking to a group of people at a networking event and says you all need to drop a clothing size, so I can help you. That could offend and lead to no business.

The same personal trainer says they help people who want to drop a dress size and stay at the new size. This time I might know someone I could refer—and if the message does apply to me I will be able to find out more.

In an online situation the same thing could be applied quite simply by asking questions.

Do you…?

If you…?

Would you…?

Questions will increase the engagement of your audience (actual or virtual) and allow people to sell themselves on your service, thus making your job much easier!

Assumptions are the termites of relationships.
—Henry Winkler

Be Authentic and Embrace Uniqueness

I once heard it said, "Be yourself—because everyone else is taken," and I liked the sentiment, so I decided to work with it. This may seem like common sense to you, yet I can tell you that I have had a few challenges with it along the way.

As I have developed as a business person (and I am hoping that some of you will relate to this!), I have learned a lot from a lot of people. From some successful people I have learned marketing strategy, mindset, and business skills—and from some people I have learned all of the above. At times, I have tried more to "be" this other person than to learn from them, which really does not work.

However, when it comes to building your business through building business relationships, it is crucial that you are "you"—that you are authentic. No one else can do what you do in exactly the way that you do it, and that is a good thing—because no one else is actually you.

Have you ever met someone that came across as a "fake" or a "pretender"? Did you want to do business with that person? Did you want to refer business to them? I would say it is unlikely.

Let's consider three examples of "famous people" who have embraced their uniqueness and who I would consider to be authentic. The disclaimer is that I have not met any of the people individually, but I hope you will see where I am going with this. When I consider these people, I just think about their levels of success and uniqueness and think I have much to learn— and much to offer everyone as a result!

Oprah Winfrey. We as the public have seen the high and low points of Oprah's life. I think it is fair to say that she is unique and embraces who she is. Here is what she has to say about the power of authenticity.

"Authenticity is about enjoying a new sense of freedom to be who we really are—ourselves, natural and without a mask in our relationships, our work, and our life. It takes courage, commitment, and depth."

Richard Branson. How can a guy who dresses in a wedding dress for a product launch and conducts multimillion dollar business deals in a hammock be anything less than unique or authentic?

Steve Jobs. One of the quotes from the late Mr. Jobs that I think is great is, "Your time is limited, so don't waste it by living someone else's life." Apple as a brand is one of the most innovative in the world, and the company is renowned for its uniqueness—and that started with Steve Jobs.

Society has a tendency to want us to fit in and be like everyone else. Yet, in business, the entrepreneurial spirit demands both authenticity and uniqueness. Both things are important as we build business relationships—which again we can liken to building personal relationships. Consider this as you evaluate your business interactions.

We Like People That Are Like Us. In many ways we really do like people that are like us as friends. We enjoy sharing experiences with our friends: doing activities or sharing a meal where we both enjoy the food and atmosphere. We might share backgrounds, experiences, education, likes and dislikes.

In business, people will often seek out others that are like them in some way when looking to buy a product or sign up for a service. Being honest about who you are and remaining authentic will allow people to make these decisions.

"He's Not the Man I Married." Have you ever heard someone say this? Often when you hear it, it is not good news. Shortly after I got married, my mum asked me whether things had changed between me and my new husband. When I said not really, I didn't understand where the conversation was going, but my mum was pleased. It is very sad, but it happens that a spouse's entire character and behaviour can change after the ceremony or after the honeymoon—and it is not a pleasant experience.

In business, people want you to be the same person before, during, and after the time they do business with you. That is only going to work if you are being authentic. If you are pretending to be someone that you are not, because you think that is how business is "supposed" to be done, you will come unstuck, as you will not be able to keep up the act long term.

Opposites Attract. Now this one may seem to go against what has gone before. If people like people that are like them, what am I talking about here? This is the point where I am really encouraging you to embrace your uniqueness. As you are your authentic self, this means you will have traits that are unique to you—traits that may be even considered "quirky."

What I am saying is to be open to the fact that by allowing people to see your uniqueness, you may be surprised at who you attract. To illustrate this, I am going to present a very unique business consultant, Leela Cosgrove:

"I was not put on Earth to help hobbyists make a few dollars. I was not put on Earth to help people make money doing s*** they hate. I was not put on Earth to wear beige, serve tea, and be nice to everyone.

I was put on this Earth to lead rampaging armies.

My army is the army of the disenfranchised. I call them "alternative entrepreneurs" —some of them are in alternative industries (bands, tattooists, fashion designers), but they are also Mormons. They're born again Christians. They're mothers and fathers. They're grandparents. They're young and single. But they all have something in common. They're looking for something different. They're tired of the wealth creation scene (or have never been interested in it). They just want information without the NLP, Hypnosis, Pretty Veneer Bull****. They're attracted to us because of the swearing— because we're different. I could never attract them by acting like everyone else—because they're not like everyone else. And neither are we."

www.leelacosgrove.com

So let's consider this. (By the way, I inputted the ****s, they were not in the original post.)

Is this brand message designed to attract everyone? Does that matter?

Yet, did you notice what is also key? She attracts people who are like her and also total opposites! Interesting…

Be yourself. The world worships the original
—Ingrid Bergman.

Your mindset is important to you in winning in life and work.

Your marketing strategy is important to you in winning in life and work.

I trust that you now see that the way you form and nurture your business relationships is also important to you in winning in life and work.

I love nothing more than being the catalyst for people to achieve even greater results in their business, so I trust that there are at least one or two "nuggets" that you can take from this chapter, implement into your business strategies, and see results.

Which strategy can you implement, tweak, or improve?

1) Open a relationship—don't close a sale
2) Give people something to talk about
3) Enjoy and join the conversation
4) Don't assume that people know anything
5) Be authentic and embrace uniqueness

I would love to connect with you further if what I have had to say resonates with you. Connect on LinkedIn or Facebook and let me know we have "met" here and how things are working for you.

Remember, it is all about the relationships—that is a great place to start.

Shift: Mindset for Success

by Kim Davey

How to Live the Life You Were Born to Live.

Kim Davey is the embodiment of living with passion.

As a young adult in New Zealand, Kim was fortunate to learn early on that living a life based on what you should do rather than what you were born to do is not the prescription for a fulfilling life.

After leaving a promising career as a lawyer to pursue her dreams of performance and travel, she achieved just that. Kim has travelled the world immersing herself in culture, new experiences, and personal development. She is currently pursuing her dream of becoming a freelance TV presenter and is founder/director of New Zealand Dance Network (NZDN).

Kim strives to inspire and empower others to seek out their true calling and follow their dreams, because as she can wholeheartedly attest, there is no greater joy than being true to who you really are.

Personal Website: www.KimDavey.TV

NZ Dance Network: www.nzdancenetwork.co.nz

Success

Q: What is success?
A: Whatever *you* define it to be.

Success is 100 percent an individual ideal. Some define it as "making the most of myself," "achieving my goals," or "getting what I want." Personally, I feel success means having the guts and the willpower to live the life I know I was born to live. We all have big dreams and ambitions for our lives. It is our duty to follow our dreams and create our dream life. Yet so many people never reach their full potential. What a waste! So why is this?

We need to understand that success is not easy! If it was, everyone would be successful. There is in fact a *huge* disparity between what most people think successful people do and what they actually do in order to make their dreams a reality. Successful people aren't lucky or necessarily more gifted, but they are the ones who are willing to commit their time, effort, and energy to achieve what it is they want. Plainly and simply they do the things other people are unwilling to do. Robert Kioysaki said, "You have to be smart. The easy days are over." So, are you *prepared and willing* to do *whatever it takes* to live the life of your dreams?

There is no one secret ingredient to success. However, one attribute does stand out above the rest: your *mindset*. The ability to *change* your current way of thinking and to embrace the proceeding chapter with an open mind will support you on your path to success. A mindset of success is driven and tenacious, positive and accountable, motivated and disciplined. This mindset needs to be involved in constant learning and the expansion of ideas, and have the attitude of gratitude. Above all it has to have a 'kick butt' and 'never say die' mentality. So come on, let's rip into the basic elements of being truly successful, and then utilize them to live the life you were born to live.

Create a Positive Mindset. We ultimately become what we think. Positivity creates more positivity and "like attracts like." Regardless of where you are now, or where you have been, we all have the ability to create a great life. To paraphrase Brian Tracy, once you change the way you think, you change your life. In order to do this, we need to change our view of the world and how we act in it. We need to focus on the good and eliminate the bad. Bad stuff will happen: it's a part of life. But what determines how well you do in life is how you react to the bad stuff. You always have a choice: you can get bitter, or you can get better. When we get better we realize that everything happens for a reason. We take what we have learnt from a situation and apply it in way that benefits us in the future. By taking this positive approach to trying situations, we develop a mindset that cannot be defeated. *No matter what happens to you, you always see the value of the lesson learnt.* Therefore you don't view the world as "out to get you" but as a huge learning ground where you get to explore, discover, and experiment with who you want to be and how you want to "play the game" of life. You then discover more ways to adapt, move forward, and achieve success in every aspect of your life.

Dream *Big* and Believe. Dreams drive life and inspire us to stay in action. If you want to be successful and live the life you want, you better start dreaming. *The BIGGER and more outrageous the better!* "If you can dream it, you can do it."—Walt Disney. You can have whatever you want. But you must believe in your dream and your ability to make it happen. Beliefs are created through our life experiences and the meanings *we* have attached to them. Therefore nothing we believe is necessarily right, wrong, or real. Our lives are determined by the boundary conditions of our thinking. So play *big* and your life will take that course. Play small and your life will stay small. "The thing always happens that you really believe in, and the belief in a thing makes it happen." —Frank Lloyd Wright. Unfortunately, the education system taught us to "get your head out of the clouds and stop dreaming." That is so wrong! In order to be successful, we must have a complete disregard for where our abilities end. We must aim beyond our current capabilities to become whoever we want to be. Years ago Victoria Beckham had the uncanny dream to be "as famous as Persil Automatic." I think she has done a pretty good job. Nothing is impossible. If you set the standards high enough for yourself you will find a way to achieve what you set out to do.

Never Be Realistic. "Being realistic is the most common path to mediocrity." —Will Smith. We are so used to our friends, parents, colleagues saying, "You have to be realistic!" I say, *screw* realistic! How does anything new get created if we are realistic? Realistic is all about being stuck in the past with old-school thinking. If Henry Ford had been realistic the world may never have seen the first motor car; if Mark Zuckerberg had been realistic we may never have had the world's largest social networking site; if I was realistic I would not be sitting here in Hawaii spending half of each year travelling the world! *Realistic kills dreams.* It kills creation. And it absolutely kills any chance of big-time success! You must look outside the box and dare to go where others are too scared to go, as this is where real life begins. Working hard to get a good job and make someone else rich is not smart. Don't let something be, just because it's always been. If you wonder why, then ask why! Too many people seek permission, follow others, and let tradition and the way it's always been dictate their lives. We need to move away from our outdated industrial-age education system's way of thinking and change how we see, talk, and behave in the world. There are no rules, only those that you impose on yourself. You can do *anything* you can imagine. Never be realistic.

Be Fearless. Too many of us live in fear. Fear of failure, fear of rejection, even fear of success! FEAR has been described as "**F**alse **E**vidence **A**ppearing **R**eal," as it is something we create in our minds when speculating on the future. It can be paralyzing, yet often when you face your fear it is never as bad as what you anticipated. Fear of failure is baseless, as it is in failure where we really learn. In the worlds of Samuel Beckett, we want to "Fail, fail again, fail better." All the time you are learning, growing, and getting a lot closer to your dreams and goals than if you hadn't attempted anything. You want to have the attitude that when you fall down, you get up and try again—over and over again. Fear of rejection can be overcome if you go out and make rejection part of the process. It is imperative you do not let the "no's" kill the goal, so be prepared for them and make it a game. Fear of success is often not obvious at first, but it can hold us back at a deep, unconscious level. In the words of Marianne Williamson, "Our deepest fear is not that we are inadequate. Our deepest fear is that we are powerful beyond measure." If this is holding you back, know that you cannot help anyone else until you first help yourself, and if you lead the way others will follow. So be fearless and go kick some butt!

Enjoy the Ride. Life should be fun! It's the journey, not the destination that really counts, so don't take anything too seriously, especially yourself. Did you know that everything we want in life we desire because we believe having it will make us feel a certain way? With everything we strive for, what we are trying to capture is the feeling that comes with having it, rather than the thing itself. So take a shortcut to happiness by having a list of all the things you love to do and do them regularly. Furthermore, your body leads your emotions. Think about it—you go for a run, you feel better. Put a smile on your face, you feel better. You dance like a crazy person, you feel better. Doing random, crazy, fun things that make us laugh improves our spirits, increases our energy, and makes life so much more fun. So get crazy! The best thing you can do in life is learn how to laugh—often and a lot. Compliment all this with an "Attitude of Gratitude." simply saying "thank you" for everything that is good, beautiful, and wonderful in your life, and you will be on fire! As I write this I am looking over the balcony onto Waikiki beach. It is a typically gorgeous Hawaiian day, blue sky, sun shining, and I have just finished singing my heart out to music from *Legally Blonde: The Musical.* I think to myself, "thank you," my life is awesome. Not everyone's cup of tea, but who cares! ***Do what makes you happy and you will love your life!***

Take Responsibility. Personal responsibility is empowering. It means taking full responsibility for who you are and what happens in your life. You do this by understanding we that attract and create everything that happens in our lives, good and bad, due to our actions or inactions. This is great news because it means we have total control to guide our lives in the direction we want. We can also change those things that are not serving us. In the wise words of Oprah's mentor Maya Angelou, "If you don't like something, change it. If you can't change it, change your attitude." We are given everything we could possibly need to live the lives we want. Resources and information abound. We can do anything, create anything, and be anything when we assume full responsibility for our lives. Only you can make or break your life—no one can live your life for you. As the saying goes: "If it's to be, it's up to me." You are here on this earth to live your own story and to create your own life. Who better than you to secure your own future? No one knows what you want more than you do. So drop your burdens, assume responsibility and get on with pursuing your dreams. ***Get up, dress up, and show up for your own life.*** Make it *brilliant*, because after all, that is the whole point of living!

Get Motivated. The universe will not provide if you sit on the couch. You must find the motivation to achieve within yourself. You cannot rely on anyone else. Ask yourself, "What would I do if I had no other option?" In the book *One Minute Millionaire* by Robert Allen and Mark Victor Hansen, a mother is forced to come up with a million dollars in a short time frame in order to keep custody of her two children. Imagine if you had that type of motivation over your head each time you were to complete a task or seek out a new opportunity! What could you achieve if you lived your life in this way? Would you do things differently? I definitely would. I know that my thinking would evolve, my risk taking increase, and I would become far more resourceful. So find someone to be successful for and raise their hopes. *Get excited for your life!* Remember that you only live once. You only get one shot. But you get to choose what path to take and you can change that path at any time. Isn't that pretty awesome? We can do whatever we want, create, learn, travel, love, give, receive, and laugh. As Danny Kaye said, "Life is a great big canvas and you should throw all the paint on it you can." If your life is not all that you want, then it's time to do something about it. Get out there and start living!

Be Disciplined, Committed, and Never Give Up. It may sound strange but in order to become successful we must first make the *decision* to be successful. When we do this we send a message of intense conviction to our entire being, and we instinctively know what to focus on. For example, a person with depression will not recover—despite all the professional and emotional support, until they themselves make the decision to get better. Once the decision is made, the focus expands and action begins. We must also have the discipline to take the required steps every single day, even when no one is looking. *A little bit, often is what it takes*. It is never the smartest who ultimately wins but the diligent student with a "never say die" mentality. In the wise words of Calvin Coolidge: "Nothing in the world can take the place of persistence. Talent will not; nothing is more common than unsuccessful men with talent. Genius will not; unrewarded genius is almost a proverb. Education will not; the world is full of educated derelicts. Persistence and determination are omnipotent." Very often it's those last troubling obstacles that represent a crazy storm before the calm. Yet that's where people quit. If you can't find the discipline inside yourself, then maybe you don't want the goal as much as you thought you did. You must decide, commit, and act on what you want in life. And never, never, never give up until you get what you want.

Be confident. Confidence literally means "your belief in yourself." Many people suffer from a lack of confidence due to past experiences and the meanings they attached to those experiences. If this is you then you need to focus on you skills and talents. Write them down, focus on what you are good at, and regain your self-belief. There are always going to be people who know more, have more, and are more experienced than you. However, there are also a lot of people out there who can appreciate you, like you, and learn from what you have to share, or enjoy what you have to give. The reason why confidence is so important is that it creates a perception in the mind of others that you know what you are doing and can therefore be trusted. People will then want to work with you and invest in you and in your dreams. Only 7 percent of communication is verbal, so we primarily demonstrate confidence in how we act. So like the age-old adage claims, "fake it till you make it." *The more action you take, the more experience you gain, and the more confident you will become.* You can also help yourself along by feeling good about the way you look. Buy some nice clothes, get your colours done, get your hair done, and look your best. First impressions are very important, so take pride in your appearance. It also gives you a nice platform on which to build your self-belief when people are constantly commenting on how nice or "good" you look. If you consciously make an effort to do things that will build your confidence, there is no end to the potential for results.

Be Authentic and Live the Life You Want. This is twofold. First, to be successful you need to be unique, which everyone is. Nobody does you like *you* do you. So don't try and be someone you are not. Sure, emulate those who have qualities and success that you would like but always ensure you remain true to who you are and what you believe. Search for *your* way to do whatever it is that will make you happy. It is about being totally authentic about who you are and what you want. Other people admire this: they like variety and something new. Secondly, with uniqueness in mind, successful people do not conform to society's preconceived notions of what is right and wrong. Everyone is different. If you want to travel the world for ten years, do it; if you want to have kids at fifty, do it; if you want to do anything, do it! Life is for living. Too many people have regrets. They live a life of what they "should" do, rather than what they want to do. ***Sometimes we must do what is best for ourselves and not what is best for everyone else.*** In reality, no one really cares what you do anyway. You may be the hot topic of conversation for ten minutes, but then everyone gets back to their own lives. Whenever you are thinking about doing something new, ask yourself, "Will I regret it if I don't do it?" If the answer is yes, then go for it!

Surround Yourself with the Right People. It has been said that "the quality of your life is determined by the mindset of the six people you spend the most time with." Scary thought? If so, there are two ways to ensure you have the right people in your life. First, get yourself a coach or mentor. Ninety nine percent of successful people have coaches and mentors who guide, challenge, and hold them accountable. A coach is there to support, encourage, and inspire you to achieve your dreams. A mentor is someone who has done what you want to do and asks you questions you wouldn't normally ask yourself to push you further than you would push yourself. Being held accountable will spur you into doing all the things you would otherwise avoid and gets you realizing your dreams much faster. When you outgrow one coach or mentor you move onto the next. Ideally you want to be bringing in an income (as a result of that coaching or mentoring) that far supersedes the investment. *"A mentor is someone who allows you to see the hope inside yourself"*—Oprah Winfrey. Second, No one achieves success without the help of a great team—but only work with the best. Work to your strengths and build a team person by person for the things you struggle with. If you surround yourself with smart, switched-on people, you will get to where you want to be a lot quicker and easier.

Ask for What You Want. And allow it to happen. This is so simple, yet so many people never do it. As the saying goes, "ask and you shall receive" and alternatively, if you don't ask, you don't get. So ask the right people. Do your research and ask the right questions to get the information you require to get to the next step. You should also ask for constructive criticism. While it is nice to be complimented, it is more helpful to seek and receive criticism. Why? First, it means the person cares enough to help you increase your game. Second, if they are going to be identifying your flaws and weaknesses, summarily correcting them will give you the edge to get you to where you want to be. ***So don't seek praise, seek criticism.*** Another great skill to master in this arena is the art of negotiation. Once you learn how to negotiate, a new world of possibilities opens up to you. As Loral Langemeier so rightly claims, "You'll never get paid what you're worth— but you do get paid what you negotiate." Mastering the art of good negotiation skills will get you far. When you think about it, you utilize these skills in all areas of your life from work to home, with yourself and your partner. Getting what you want is ultimately dependent on how well you can negotiate what you want. So learn how to do it well. Read biographies on the likes of Richard Branson and Donald Trump and take courses on negotiation technique. It could make or save you thousands.

Listen to Your Intuition (Gut Instincts). Ok, this is a biggie. We all have this ability, no arguments. The only difference is that some of us are aware of it and use it while some blatantly ignore it. Your "gut instinct" is that feeling you get in your tummy when you have to make a decision about something, and it is either telling you it is right or wrong. Many, many, many famous people talk about the importance of listening to and following your intuition in all aspects of life, both personal and professional. Even Albert Einstein said ***"The only real valuable thing is intuition."*** Intuition is your innermost desires, beliefs, and feelings speaking to you from your unconscious. It is always right. "The power of intuitive understanding will protect you from harm until the end of your days." —Lao Tzu. I want to share a story about a recent time in my life where my intuition potentially saved me. Whenever I am in my hometown of Napier, New Zealand I always go on a specific hill walk. This particular day I was approaching the corner to the steepest street when I got this overwhelming feeling to avoid it, turn back, and walk through the gardens instead. I had never done this before, but I listened to my gut and went through the gardens. As I walked, I heard two gun shots coming from the steepest street behind the trees. As I walked out the top of the gardens an armed policeman came running over to me yelling to get out. A crazed man had just shot a civilian and shot dead a policeman on the steepest street. This kind of thing *never* happens in Napier. What followed was a three-day lockdown of the hill and national media attention. I had been seconds away from being caught in the middle of it, but my intuition saved me. Imagine if I hadn't listened. So whenever you feel lost, or unsure, be still and quiet. Your intuition will give you the answers you seek.

Educate Yourself on a Daily Basis. All successful people know that education does not end after high school or university. In fact this is where real education begins. Personal development in the form of books, audio, DVD's, and seminars are the way to fill your mind with powerful information on the topics of mindset, success, money, relationships, health, spirituality, and many more. Too many people are unaware that this information exists, because it is not taught in school. So Google these amazing thought leaders for motivation and inspiration; Tony Robbins, John D. Martini, Chris Howard, Les Brown, Zig Ziglar, T. Harv Eker, and Jim Rohn. Look at Abraham Hicks for understanding the purpose of life at www.abraham-hicks.com. For true health and well-being you cannot surpass the incredible Don Tolman at www.dontolmaninternational.com. These people have literally changed my life and got me to where I am today…writing this chapter for one! I am five years out of university, and while I learnt a lot on specific subjects—namely law, politics and theatre—I can honestly say I have learnt one hundred times more about myself, life, and how to be successful from the personal development seminars, CD's, and books. I truly believe that *you can and will be more successful in life with a personal development education than a university degree.* Personal development equips you with real life skills that you need in order to create the life you want, not the one a boss dictates to you. So find yourself some personal development material, devour it, and let me know how it changes your thinking and therefore your life!

Practice Well-Being. When it comes to making the most of life you can't do much without your health. So it is important you create the right foundations to build your dreams so that you can enjoy the fruits of your labour. It begins with eating right, getting appropriate sleep and exercise, but also following the "Seven Principles of Health" as defined by the incredible Don Tolman. They include getting enough fresh air, filtered water, natural sunlight, movement, whole foods (natural and organic fruit and vegetables), nontoxic relationships, and a passion for something. (Read more at www.thedontolman.com). It is also important to be happy with where you live. For example, if you live in a predominantly grey, rainy location, and this type of weather gets you down, move to somewhere sunny. If you are away from family and miss them, move to be closer. You may be thinking, "but I can't move because of x, y, or z." You actually can, if you think outside the box and want it bad enough, it will become a reality. If you *go to the place where you "flow"* you will feel much happier with your life. Finally, be organized. The more organized you are in your day, the more you will accomplish and the more likely you will succeed. So make sure you have what you need to do so: smart phone, laptop, and software. Don't waste precious time and energy trying to replace what technology can do for you in a second! If you lay the correct foundations you will reap the rewards of a healthy, positive life.

Meditate. Meditation is today widely practiced by many successful people to calm the mind and relax the body. It is not weird or scary as some may believe. All you do is sit in a comfortable position, usually on the floor, and focus on nothing but your breathing. When your mind begins to wander, you return your focus to your breathing. Afterwards you feel inner peace, calm, and connected to your intuition. Twenty minutes a day is all it takes to work wonders in your life. If you want to take it a step further, you can try meditation retreats such as the Vipassana ten-day silent meditation held virtually everywhere on the planet. See www.dhamma.org. If you are unsure about meditation, begin with another technique called "Morning Pages," created by Julia Cameron, author of *The Artist's Way*. "Morning Pages" are three pages of longhand, stream-of- consciousness writing, done first thing in the morning. They are about anything and everything that crosses your mind—and they are for your eyes only. More often than not "Morning Pages" are negative, fragmented, repetitive, or bland. Worrying about your job, the laundry, or the weird look your friend gave you—all that distracts you from your creativity, so you use these pages to dump out your negativity, and move on with your day with a freer spirit. Both these techniques *release the mind from all the clutter* to allow you to get on with your day with clarity and focus.

Set and Achieve Your Goals. Goals are so important as they give our lives purpose. To be successful in achieving your goals, you must male them totally congruent with who you are—meaning that your head's and heart's desires must match so that they "feel right." Start by clarifying what you want to achieve in each area of your life—health, relationships, career, money, and spirituality, thinking; Where do I want to be this time next month? Next season? Next year? **If you don't know what you want just yet, who cares!** Write some goals that move you out of your comfort zone to try new things. It's all about refining. Work out what you don't want, then look at what you do want. Write down these goals, following the SMART goal-setting formula because "A goal properly set is halfway reached." —Zig Ziglar.

S = Your goal must be Specific.
M= You must be able to Measure your progress.
A= Your goal must be Attainable.
R= Your goal must be realistic (Realistic by the date you know it will occur. Not necessarily by today's circumstances. So *dream big!*).
T = Your goal must have a Time deadline/future date.

Once your goals are written down, you can adjust them throughout your journey to cater to your changed desires. As long as the goal is there, there is no limit to your achievement. You must refer to them often, with positive energy and visualize them occurring. More than anything, you must become the type of person who gets to live that moment.

Understand and Practice Visualization. Did you know that *the mind cannot tell the difference between something real or imagined?* Read that again! So when we visualize ourselves achieving our goals and inject feeling and emotion into it, the mind believes it has already happened. So when it comes time to actually take the steps to achieve the goal in real life, the mind finds it so much easier because it feels like it has done it before. Try it! In the words of Clement Stone, "What the mind can conceive, the mind can achieve." When visualizing your goal, imagine yourself at the point where you know it has occurred. For example, if you want an overseas holiday, you might imagine yourself paying for the airfare, getting onto the plane, or unpacking at the hotel. Pour as much positivity, colour, and intensity into that image as you can. First see it through your own eyes and then take a snapshot of it. The more real you make it, the more your mind will "know" it is real. Also, create a vision board: a cardboard collage of magazine clippings or photos, of all the things you want to achieve in your life, e.g. beautiful house, happy relationships, fit and healthy body, etc. Hang it on the wall above your desk or somewhere you will always see it. The vision board acts as a constant reminder of what it is you are working towards and your mind will start creating ways to get it. Every time you look at it, you need to feel positive, love, fullness, success, and imagine that these are already yours. The famous author John Assaraf had a multimillion dollar home on his vision board and years later when unpacking boxes after moving into a new home he found his vision board and on it was *the* house he had just moved into! So kick-start achieving your goals faster through visualization.

Focus on the Things That Matter. Once you know what you want, have set your goals, and begun visualizing them, it is imperative you focus on doing what it takes to achieve them. You do not need to know "how," just go as far as you can see, and then you will see what comes next. Create PRD's (Performance Results Descriptions), objectives to be achieved in a certain timeframe. Split up your goals into bite-sized chunks, so you know what you need to focus on first. Our focus then needs to be shifted to the present. Not the past or future, but what we need to do today. Focus itself is mental discipline. *What we focus on expands.* The only thing we can control is what we do from moment to moment, so find a way to eliminate distractions, the nemesis of focus. Focus on one thing at a time and don't spread yourself too thin. We are all guilty of jeopardizing our success by trying to do too much. A good friend once said to me "If you were a voyager on a ship looking for land for months and finally one day saw it, you wouldn't zig zag your way there in case you discovered some other piece of land, you would keep your eye on it and sail directly there!" So remember to always keep your eye on the end result.

Take Action to Get Results. Once you have set your goals and are focused on achieving them, you must spend most of your time taking action. As the great saying by Nolan Bushnell states, "Everyone who's ever taken a shower has an idea. It's the person who gets out of the shower, dries off, and does something about it that makes a difference." There is no point setting goals, visualizing, staying focused, and never doing anything to make your dreams a reality. You won't get anywhere. Action is the key to success! So look at your goals, break them into PRD's and start work on them *today.* **It's all about gaining traction.** You only have to see the first step; after taking it, the next will appear. As long as you take each step, as it come's you will gain momentum and your goal will eventuate. The secret is to keep moving. Life is pretty fast paced these days, and you need to move your butt to get ahead. Don't wait for the best opportunity, the one you have *is* the opportunity. Don't wait for everything to be perfect, because perfect doesn't exist. As Donald Trump says, "In the end, you're measured not by how much you undertake but by what you finally accomplish." So get out of your head and into action. While you are at it, strive to be the best by exceeding all expectations. While mediocrity is the norm, those that produce excellence and exceed expectations prevail. In the words of Steve Jobs, creator of Apple, "Become a yardstick of quality. Some people aren't used to an environment where excellence is expected." So get to it!

Life is funny. We all have twenty-four hours in a day. Yet some people achieve so much more than others. Think of the likes of Mother Theresa, Gandhi, and Martin Luther King Jr.: they all had the same amount of time as the rest of us, yet they made a distinctly profound impact with their lives. It all comes down to *mindset*, the willingness to do those things written above that most people are unprepared to do.

These include, but are not limited to: creating the life you want instead of allowing life to happen to you; focusing on the positive aspects of every situation; dreaming big and believing in your goals; questioning why things are the way they are, and setting your own boundaries of what is right; never succumbing to what others believe is realistic; being fearless of everything that appears to stand in your way; enjoying the incredible ride that is life, and always taking responsibility for whatever happens; being motivated, disciplined, committed, and maintaining a never-day-die mentality; being confident and authentic in living the life you want; purposely surrounding yourself with the right people, including coaches and mentors; asking for what you want; constantly working to educate yourself, practicing well-being and the calming effects of meditation; and lastly, setting and achieving your goals through visualization, focus, and taking action.

So success doesn't belong to the smartest or fastest person. Success belongs to those who get up every single day and make the conscious decision to be, do, and have more in life. When we commit to this decision and naturally gravitate to all that is written above, life begins to change. We think and see differently and produce significantly different results. So I challenge you today to choose one or more of the above attributes or practices you currently do not utilize and incorporate them into your life. Watch as they make a profound impact on your success and the way that you view the world. Continue to add more and more until you are able to craft the life you were born to live. It will happen, so get to it!

Moving on from Loss: Creating the Impossible?

by Ian Douglas

Ian has spent most of his life as a teacher, working mostly with children who do not speak English as their first language. He has now reached the age of sixty-five and is still enjoying tutoring youngsters in English.

He has always enjoyed outdoor activities, particularly sailing and mountain walking, as well as exploring and learning languages. He has taught English in both France and Italy and still spends a lot of time in Italy with his Italian wife. He loves the stage too, especially comedy, and made regular appearances as Shakespeare clowns in his youth. Ever since he studied ecology for his degree, he has been passionate about looking after the environment, and was coordinator of his local Friends of the Earth in the late eighties. Most of all, he loves learning and admits to an addiction to historical and scientific documentaries.

He has a young family, and aspires to create an income that will provide for all their needs. He is very aware that the death of his father when he was eight, as well as other losses he incurred when he was younger, have contributed to difficulties he has had in letting go and moving on. His mission is to teach others what he has learned from his experiences, to help them to overcome their own losses and move on in the most effective way they can.

If you are worried about retirement, redundancy, or losing your home, this chapter is for you. If you have already experienced such losses, or any others for that matter, this material is still relevant for you.

I will tell you my story, and show you how your worries, and possible inability to act, may be based on losses you have undergone in the past, and how these losses can negatively impact your decisions today.

I will show you how I have learnt to overcome these losses, and how I am better able to do things I never thought possible.

I will show you how you can do this too, guiding you through some of the basic principles you need to understand, and how you can use them to create a far richer and more fulfilling life than you ever dreamed.

Have you ever thought, "I'd like to do this," or "My dream is to do that," but never really thought it was possible? This chapter is for you too.

<u>My Story</u>

We lost my father suddenly when I was eight and my sister was six. My mother was totally distraught, particularly as my father had taken his own life, so you can imagine what beliefs and emotions she was experiencing. I don't remember much from when I was eight, but clearly recall her coming into my room, tears streaming down her cheeks, and telling me that my father was never coming back.

The next thing I recall was being in the living room with my grandparents later that same night, and being whisked off by taxi to their house in another part of London. My sister and I never set foot in the house again, nor did we ever go back to our school or see our friends. In a nutshell, we had lost everything and everybody we had ever known, apart from each other and our (relatively distant) extended family.

Very soon, we were in a new school, quickly making new friends, and moving forward with our lives. In a strange way, I was quite content. My new friends had completely replaced the old ones—I didn't need them anymore. In some ways, it is very easy to adapt to a new situation when you are young. For a long time, though,

I secretly hoped they had lied to me, and that my father was in prison, although I knew this was just wishful thinking.

However, despite my resilience, many years later I became aware that this traumatic event had left deep scars, and that I had a more or less compulsive tendency to behave in a way that I now recognise was self-defeating. As a young man, I used to describe myself as "congenitally late," meaning that I always stayed where I was until the very last minute before moving on. I never left any leeway for traffic jams or buses being late, so I rarely arrived anywhere on time. Not only did I beat myself up for this, but was constantly criticised or punished by those in authority. In the early sixties, pastoral care in schools hadn't been invented. The attitude was, "You've been late all week, so you're suspended." I found it excruciatingly difficult to leave friends at school or university to go home, as I did to go to bed, get up, or leave the house. No wonder, when leaving or moving on unconsciously meant the loss of my father, my friends, my home, as well as a mentally stable mother! Even now, in my sixties, I still have a tendency to stay up late, get up late, and overstay my welcome, although at least I am aware of the origins of this behaviour, so can choose to act differently if I want.

Being sent away for a fortnight at a time with my sister, to give my mother a break during the school holidays, made me massively homesick. The first time, we were driven in my great-aunt's friend's Morris Minor to a kind of *colonie de vacances* in Selsey. (This was before I'd ever heard of Patrick Moore, although a visit to his house would have made the heartache bearable!) I did in fact enjoy a lot of the activities, and spent a lot of time pretending to speak French to some of the many French children there, knowing perfectly well that what I was saying would make no sense to them whatsoever! The overwhelming feeling, however, was one of loneliness, with an underlying fear that I would never go home again—likewise when we were packed off to stay with the Jays, my aunt's ex-neighbours, a lovely old couple who had moved to Herne Bay. It was only a couple of hours away on the train, but it seemed like the other end of the universe, and I remember my mother coming to visit at the weekend, and telling her I wanted to come home.

Don't get me wrong. I'm not blaming the past for the way I became. We *all* have similar stories—events that have scarred us and contributed to making us who and what we are today. And many of these subtly undermining events, just like mine, involve loss. If you can answer "yes" to any of these questions, you have suffered a potentially damaging loss:

Have you lost a parent, a son or daughter, a brother, sister, or spouse?

Did your parents split up when you were still dependent on them?

Have you ever lost your home, particularly against your will, such as eviction or repossession?

Have you ever been in local authority care?

Did you ever have to move school?

Have you ever had to move country, particularly as a refugee?

Have you ever lost a job that you wanted to keep?

The common denominator in all these situations is that the loss is not only unwanted, but something that rocks the very foundation of our security, our trust in either ourselves, other people, or life itself—or even all three. When we undergo such events as children, we are resilient and cope, often "too well." The feelings get buried, stunting our spiritual and emotional growth, and often causing us serious illness in later life.

But we are not victims, and we must *never* see ourselves as victims.

By this I mean that we **must not blame our past or anybody in our past** for the way we are now. We must not blame anybody, **including ourselves**, for **anything**!

In fact, life has given us exactly what we need—not necessarily what we want—providing us with the **learning** we **need** to move forward and become the best we can.

The fact is that we **can overcome anything** that has happened to us in our past. Just look at the thousands of people in this country alone who have gotten into drugs or gangs, done time in prison, and been on the verge of despair, **and have turned their lives around**, to become some of the most **inspirational** and **effective** people around. People such as Chris Preddie, who was awarded the OBE in 2012 for having turned his back on drug dealing after his brother was shot, and becoming a leading light working with ex-offenders; or Lynette Moreau, who spent twenty years as an intravenous methamphetamine addict, and is now a college professor with three degrees and two beautiful grandchildren; or Spencer West, who lost both his legs at the age of five, and then climbed Kilimanjaro in his wheelchair. The list goes on, and on, and on…

How Did It Affect Me?

Getting stuck and finding it difficult to move forward can affect us in all sorts of ways.

As I mentioned before, I found it difficult to move out of whatever situation I found myself in, be it the company of friends, sitting in front of the television in the evening, or enjoying my morning dreams in the comforting warmth of my bed. Nowadays, I need to beware of playing games on the computer in the evening, as I am well inside my comfort zone and have a tendency to say to myself, almost unconsciously, "Just one more," continuing on until well after midnight, despite its consequent toll on my energy the next day. This may, of course, be more linked to the way that young people invariably get hooked by computer games when left to their own devices, although, in my case at least, I can also see a connection to the losses I received when my father died. Maybe young people getting stuck on computer games are themselves compensating for a loss involving their own parents in their infancy?

Something else that afflicts me to this day is the unwillingness to let go of the day job. In some ways, this can be a good thing, as it provides me with a steady income, so I don't need to worry so much about my finances. The problem here is that my continued employment means (a) the fact that I'm still earning means that I don't have enough pain to create an alternative income, (b) that I'm not freeing up the time that I need to in order to develop my business and (c) I'm not making the best contribution I could to the world. As far as point (a) is concerned, it is a fact that the majority of people who have made a huge impact in the world have made their most important decisions from an extremely painful situation. I think of people like Anthony Robbins, Chris Howard, Nelson Mandela, and Mother Teresa. It is pain, whether financial, spiritual, or otherwise that has got them all moving, motivating them to change their own lives so that they can help others to change theirs. Sadly, it is often illness that creates the pain, that makes the afflicted patient say, "Enough! I *must* do what I can to change this situation." Cancer or diabetes, for example, may be the spur that gets the individual to change our diet/lifestyle.

Letting go of Employment

As a teacher, I have had to apologise in the third leaving speech at the same school for repeatedly leaving and then coming back. Embarrassingly for me, the staff had clubbed together each time for the usual leaving present, although it did get smaller and less valuable each time! At the next school I worked in, I didn't make the same mistake—I made a different one. I hung on and on for twenty years, long after I was really giving of my best. This was where I retired, or rather took my pension, and then promptly went back for four days a week! I wanted to use my day off to develop a coaching business but almost gave up, as there were always distractions.

Besides, although I was vaguely aware that the money was slowly slipping away, I was still too much in my comfort zone to be willing to make the bold, confident steps I needed to.

But it was still scary! Did you know that first-time mothers in their late thirties are officially termed "elderly" by the NHS? I know this because my wife was thirty-nine when she was pregnant with our first child. If she was elderly, I was positively geriatric, being fifty-one when my daughter was born. Not only that, we went on to have a second child, a son, who was born when I was just a couple of weeks short of my fifty-fourth birthday. No wonder the idea of letting go of my day job was scary! At the time of writing, I'm sixty-five and my son is just about to start secondary school. It does, however, frequently occur to me that I've conveniently and unconsciously set up an *excuse* for not giving up the day job. At one level, if I don't stay in my comfort zone (employment), I won't be taking responsibility for looking after my young family.

I am, however, now in the fortunate position of being able to work exactly when I want to, provided it's during the school day. Clearly, the more hours I work, the more I get paid, so I can't afford to take too many days off. I am, however, using this flexibility to begin to develop my own business. Although I'm still in my comfort zone, I can take baby steps to leave it, and know that, even if I fall, I can pick myself up and go back to Mummy!

I am very aware, however, that you, dear reader, are probably not in this privileged position. I see it as an honour and duty to encourage you to do whatever you need to in order to fulfill your purpose and your destiny. Of that, I will say more later. Suffice it to say that we all have a purpose, and that right now it may not be obvious to you. Indeed, it may well be buried under your own personal rubbish tip. Have you ever looked for a needle in a haystack? Don't worry, it's not as difficult as that. The needle is actually quite big and shiny, although you may need to wash off the filth and slime before you spot it!

How Long Has It Lasted?

One thing that is very clear to me is that the effects of my father's death have lasted throughout my life thus far, and. I don't expect them to ever disappear completely, although now I am more in control of them than when I was young. I am also aware that this major event was only one of a huge number of events that have affected my life at a subconscious level. The fact is that everything that happened to me as a baby has left an imprint on my unconscious, just as everything in *your* infancy has done. Some of those events, which are not accessible to recall because of our lack of awareness when they happened, were no doubt pretty powerful in their impact too. This brings into play the power of parents to affect their small children, and their responsibility for the way they behave and speak to their children. That, however, is for another book. The important thing here is that babyhood memories are practically inaccessible at a conscious level, while the effects of later events can be accessed more easily, hence my awareness of the effects of the events surrounding my father's death.

From a very early age I have been aware of things I wanted to change in my life. I have always had some dissatisfaction with the way my life seemed to be heading, although at another level I was quite happy.

When I was deciding which degree course to follow, I drifted into teaching because, I was persuaded that, as teaching was a steady job, I would never be out of work. Not, you notice, that I had a passion for children or for my subject. I was "kind of" happy with teaching, as I enjoyed working with young people, as well as the relationships I formed with my colleagues, and never really considered leaving the safety of my job.

What kept me going was the fact that I was never really content, and was always willing to take opportunities that presented themselves. For example, my teaching colleague wanted to work on the stage, and I accompanied him to the Tower Theatre in Islington, one of the most professional amateur companies in London, for an audition. Next thing I knew, *I* had been cast as Verges in *Much Ado About Nothing*, which was the start of several years being regularly cast as the Shakespeare clown. My colleague went on to drama school and is now a professional actor, while I never really took it seriously—or rather never took my talents seriously. After all, how could I even consider leaving the safety of my job?

What did make a huge difference to me was taking a personal development course called "Awakening the Mind," created by an organisation now known as More To Life. Here I learned about my "mind-talk" and what I could do to put it in check, about dealing with resentment, about venting our anger in a safe way, and most important, validating the person we fundamentally are, and how we truly want to be in the world. Not only this, but I was also given the opportunity to take another weekend course to teach "The Power of Self-Esteem," which, being a teacher, I immediately knew I wanted to do, as I knew how valuable it had been to learn the More To Life principles at my original weekend. Over the following months and years, I took other More To Life courses, focused on relationships, sexuality, money, and willingness, among others, and took several roles on various training teams, thus developing my leadership skills. I also taught their "Power of Purpose" course, which provided some highly effective processes to help participants achieve what they want. In addition, I became involved in the support community for More To Life, which helped me develop my leadership skills.

When my children finally put in an appearance, however, my focus inevitably changed, and I stopped working on training teams and teaching courses, although I still continued to use the invaluable processes I had learnt.

As the twenty-first century dawned, my wife and I both decided we wanted to become life coaches. We had both had counseling training as part of our academic studies, and were interested in helping people to make life-changing decisions. My wife thought counseling was a very demanding path to follow, and we both wanted to create an income at a time when it suited us. Women with children will certainly understand this, and my son was still in primary school when I reached retirement age. Between us, we knew we would need an alternative income. So off we went to train with the Coaching Academy.

Although we were confident we would be effective coaches, we hadn't reckoned on the business of getting clients and how we would market our services. Neither of us had been in business before. As a teacher in state schools, I had always been an employee with no real idea or interest in how businesses worked.

What helped us to get moving was two tickets that Jonathan Jay, the founder and then-owner of the Coaching Academy, gave us. They were for Christopher Howard's "Breakthrough to Success." Here was a totally different style of personal development course from those of More To Life, based on the principles of NLP (Neuro-Linguistic Programming) and hypnosis. Again, very powerful, but this time based far more on subliminal effects. It took two more advanced courses to reveal the "secrets" behind BTS. As with More To Life, I followed up not only with more advanced courses, but also with working on training "crews," again learning valuable processes that helped me in identifying and achieving my goals. It was here that I also began to hone my speaking skills, and I am now one of the privileged few who are not petrified at the very thought of getting up on stage and speaking to an audience.

I have aimed at my "private victory," as Stephen Covey calls working on one's own beliefs and behaviours, which now gives me the opportunity (and I would say duty and responsibility) to come out into the world and create my "public victory." Since my teenage years when it was very limited, my confidence has grown, sometimes in slow motion, sometimes faster, often threatening to shoot through the roof.

What Did I Want to Change and Why?

Although I'd always had ideas of things I'd like to do and might well be good at, such as writing a book, writing comedy, performing on stage, or becoming prime minister, as a young man I put these down as "delusions of grandeur." I didn't know anyone who had gotten anywhere near achieving any of them. I would clearly be out of my league, or so I thought. Not that I ever told anybody, as I was sure they'd think I was mad, so I never allowed myself the possibility of even thinking about asking anyone for support. Even now, I know it is an important principle *not* to tell most people you know of your "crazier" plans and ideas, because 99 percent of the time, they'll just put you down. Above all, don't tell your family or your "best friends," as they'll either want to protect you from yourself and the big bad world, or they'll try and stop you from "getting above your station"—after all, who do you think you are anyway?

My worst enemy, however, was not my family or my friends, but myself. So please don't blame your family or friends either, because you, too, are your own worst enemy, just like everyone else. But that's just the bad news! The good news is that you have the power to be your own best friend. In fact, if you're not your own best friend, you're not doing yourself justice.

Whatever you see as your purpose in life, you can achieve it. You may well need to make some detours on the way—welcome them, as they are there to teach you something new. One thing is for sure: a supportive community is beyond value, just as the mutual support given to one another by the writers of this book. Take the opportunity to be part of such a community, and you'll be eternally grateful.

Have You Achieved What You Set Out To Do?

The truth is I'm still in the process and always will be. I see the whole of life as a process. You have to live it day by day, taking what life brings you, moment to moment. Life can be changed in an instant, just as it was for my family and me when my father died. We all need to know this, and be as prepared as we can for any eventuality. Isn't that why we take out insurance?

Several years ago, I created a vision for myself, where I decided what I wanted to achieve by the end of my life. I learned about the "rocking chair test," in which I imagined how I would feel if I stayed as I was, not achieving anything new, sitting in my rocking chair, or worse, lying on my deathbed, at the end of my life. The regret of knowing how much I could have contributed to the world, and how I had totally failed to do any of it, provided the pain I needed to take the next part of the test. In this, I pictured myself having written my books, and communicated with people in as many different ways as I could. I imagined everything I had done to reach where I was. What a difference!

Later, I learned that visualisation was most effective if I saw myself in a position where I was receiving accolades from others, such as at an award ceremony, where I had the people around me with whom I really wanted to spend the rest of my life. I saw myself with my loved ones in the house of my dreams, or rather in the garden in the warm sunshine, with magnificent views of nature for everyone to enjoy. I also learned to feel, hear, smell, and taste *to the full* everything in my ideal scenario.

If you haven't done this yourself, believe me, it feels wonderful. You may think, "No, this is just wishful thinking! I'm deluding myself." Yes, it is wishful thinking, but you are *not* deluding yourself. In fact, if you don't do something similar, I guarantee that you'll continue to drift through life from day to day without any clear idea of where you are going. If you do a thorough visualisation, where you turn up the brightness, the contrast, the volume, the tastes, and the smells, you will *begin* to attract to yourself what you hold most dear.

Every now and then, I visualise again. I can do it instantly as I've done it before, as it's my own creation, and just as important, I *experience it fully.*

This is the message of *The Secret*, and it's true. But what the book doesn't tell you is that this is *only the first step*. Yes, of course you were sceptical about *The Secret*, because you're worldly wise and you know that this can't be all you have to do. And of course you were right.

You need to take action. *If you don't take action, nothing will happen.* Life will just carry on as before, with the odd wake-up call along the way, and *life will leave you behind!*

Is that what you want? Of course not! After all, you are still reading this, and you wouldn't be doing that if you didn't want to succeed, would you? Besides, *you know you will do what it takes*, won't you?

What to Do Next

So let's get down to it. Here is a proven method that most successful people use. It may seem counter-intuitive, but it works.

Always Start with the End in Mind

You know where you want to end up, so start there.

Then ask yourself what you need to do in the final five/ten/twenty years of your life to reach your dream. Use whatever timescale is appropriate to you. (Most older people will of necessity choose a shorter timescale than younger people.)

I started with an assumption that I would live to ninety (and still be healthy!). Of course, this may well not happen, but if I visualise myself at ninety, I believe I am more likely to get there. I could visualise myself as older, but the purpose of the exercise is to make sure I do what I need to well before I die, and if I give myself too much time, I'm more likely to drift.

Choose the Age You Will Be in Yor Visualisation

What are the last things you need to do to achieve what you visualise? I decided that, in my eighties, I need to write my masterpiece as well as appearing in front of the public as much as possible. In fact, I need to be writing and speaking as much as possible during my seventies too. Notice that I don't expect to write my masterpiece before I'm eighty, or even before my late eighties, which takes the pressure off the earlier years, as I'm not making such great demands on myself.

Now we come to the business end: the next five to ten years. Please be aware of a fundamental principle that I first heard from Anthony Robbins—that we can achieve much less in a year than we expect to. Conversely, we can achieve much more than we expect in ten years. We seem to forget that ten is *ten times* as much as one!

Expect to Have Achieved Most of Your Goals in Ten Years' Time

Aim to do lots of things towards your major focus. There is no reason why you shouldn't achieve them within a ten-year time scale. I would encourage you, in fact, to try achieving in the next ten years virtually *everything* you want to before the end of your life. If you do, you may well find that life conjures up *more opportunities and ideas* that you haven't even thought of yet. After all, twenty-five years ago, I hadn't even imagined the possibility of sitting at a computer typing this, then magically being able to send it to someone on the other side of the world!

Brainstorm Everything You Want to Achieve in Your Life.

Be bold! At this stage, don't edit anything. Enjoy it. Write it all down. It may help you to divide up your life into different areas first, such as career, relationships, health, etc., in order to create added focus.

Now for the **next five years**.

Clearly, you're not going to do all that in the next five years, so this is where you start editing and selecting what you want to have achieved in those first five years. Notice I say the *first* five years, rather than the next five years. After all, the past is past, and *today* is the beginning of the rest of your life. Remember, too, that five is half of ten, so you should aim to achieve roughly half of what you're intending to do in the first ten years.

Now decide what you're going to achieve in the **next two years**.

You'll find that, as you come closer to the present day, you'll be expecting less of yourself, and it will look more achievable and realistic.

Now, what are you going to achieve in the **next year**?

Then, go for the **next six months**.

Then **three months.**

One month.

This week.

Divide this week up. What are you going to do each day? Don't be too ambitious—ambition is for the long term. You know how to get to the top of the mountain, one step at a time. But do make sure that you take *one* important step towards your goal every day. Brian Tracey says it in the title of his best-known book, *Eat That Frog!* Make sure you do the most important thing *first*, and you can relax for the rest of the day!

At the end of the week, **review it**. Did you achieve everything you intended to? If not, why not? Were your goals realistic? If not, how can you make them realistic? Or would another strategy work better? Then decide what actions you're going to take the following week.

Keep reviewing, acting, and moving forward. You may find you've stopped. If so, what happened? What do you need to do to get back on track? Just keep going.

Coaching

A coach is an invaluable tool for helping you achieve what you want. What the coach does is listen to you, help you to make your own decisions, contribute ideas you may not have thought of and, most importantly, hold you to account. If you haven't done what you said you would, your coach will help you see why, examine various possibilities, decide what you really want, make fresh decisions, and move forward.

The fact is, of course, that life is fluid, constantly giving us new challenges to respond to. The important thing is to keep the end in mind, and to regularly reexamine what we are going to do to achieve that end.

Clearing

I mentioned earlier in this chapter, when talking about what I had learnt with More To Life, the idea of "mind-talk." This is known by many names: self-talk, internal chatter, internal dialogue, and many more. The number of names given to this phenomenon goes to show

how much it is recognised across the board by those who have studied human behaviour. It consists of the messages our unconscious mind gives us that make us feel in a particular way, and thus behave in a particular way. Some of these unconscious beliefs about ourselves, others, and the world are positive and upholding, based primarily on the love we have received when we were very young. Some, however, are extremely negative and destructive, and trip us up at the slightest opportunity. If, for example, we have constantly been treated as a nuisance by our parents when we were in our infancy, we unconsciously and automatically believe that we are a nuisance—to everyone in all circumstances, as the unconscious mind cannot distinguish between different people and situations and creates a *universal* belief. Whenever a situation presents itself that our unconscious mind recognises, the mind-talk *automatically* kicks in completely below the radar so that we are totally unaware of it. Imagine what sort of decisions you will make around other people if you hold an unconscious belief that you are a nuisance—or unworthy, hateful, selfish, or unlovable. Yes, we *all* have unconscious negative beliefs that sneak in and trip us up. No amount of positive parenting will eliminate them completely, although it is vitally important that parents do recognise the effects of their behaviour and language on their children. We are, after all, our children's first models—as babies and toddlers they look up to as almost as gods—so what we *do* is more important than what we *say*. However, what we say *about them* has a massive effect, as they believe it implicitly, and as small children cannot distinguish between what their parents say and the real truth. It all goes straight into the unconscious, and will trip them up until the day they die, unless they learn to recognise it and challenge it. And the truth is that *everybody* wants the best for themselves and their loved ones, even if their behaviour suggests otherwise. You don't need to believe this, but you do need to believe the truth about *you*.

Ok, so all this negativity gets put in place when we're babies and toddlers, before we have much of a handle on what we and the world are all about, right? Well, not quite. It's not that simple. You see, because these beliefs are unconscious, they keep compounding whenever something happens that triggers them. And the bigger the event that triggers them, the greater will be the damage to our unconscious mind.

Let's go back to the big loss of my life. In many ways, as much as I missed him and had to contend with the effect on my mother, the loss of my father did not have a huge negative impact on my life, as such negative mind-talk had not been put in place from my infancy. I had, however, missed my mother when she spent time in hospital when I was a toddler. I didn't remember it consciously, although I know it happened, as I have been told about it. The impact of the losses surrounding my father's death merely compounded the beliefs I had put in place about myself being left as a toddler by the most important person in my life.

So for me, since taking Awakening the Mind, it has always been very clear that I sometimes need to clear "mind-talk" around the isse of being left, around loss. It is only by doing this that I can come to terms with even minor losses in my adult life. Joe Vitale, one of the contributors to *The Secret,* suggests several methods of clearing. One of these is the Ho-oponopono method he learned from Dr. Hew Len, in which one recites simply, "I love you," "I'm sorry," "Please forgive me," and "Thank you." These reflect the fundamental attitudes we all need to hold towards life. In his books, Joe Vitale talks about how Dr. Hew Len cured *all* the inmates of the Hawaii institution for the criminally insane by simply reading their clinical notes and reciting "I love you," etc. and without meeting any of them!

Although I am not looking for such wide-ranging results myself, I often use this method myself, particularly as I can take as long or as short a time as I want on it. I also use some of Christopher Howard's NLP techniques taught to me by Johnnie Cass, such as the Decision Destroyer.

I do, however, still also practise what I consider to be the in-depth method of clearing I learned from More To Life, which involves reliving the offending event, feeling the associated emotions, listening for and verifying the internal chatter. This is wonderfully liberating. I then often go on to write what is true about myself in this situation, and finally make some clear choices about how I want to act. There is a huge difference in quality between making clear choices based on what we truly desire and the feeling of "having to" take the same actions. Always beware of using the words "have to," "must," "ought to," and "should." They can be extremely pernicious, particularly when applied to our own motivation. If you make something a "*must*," make sure you are clear about what you really want, and base it on that.

An Invitation

If you want to know more about how best to confront these big decisions, please check out my website: www.moving-on.co.uk.

You will also find links there to the organisations I have mentioned in this chapter.

Whatever you choose to do, always remember who you fundamentally are—a person of great value—and that you do what you do for the best of motives. Most of all, have faith in what happens to you and those around you, and learn life's lessons.

I wish you well on your journey.

Five Pillars for Supporting Women to Get Fit to Win

by Claudia Crawley

Claudia Crawley is a life coach, colour coach, and founder and director of Winning Pathways Coaching. She is also an Arbonne independent consultant. Her background is in criminal justice and social care and latterly in social work management. Throughout, she developed an approach that she uses in this work, which has enabled first her staff and currently her clients to move from now to next, by building greater choices and independence. It is based on values of equality, empowerment, and self-determination.

In 2010 when she founded Winning Pathways Coaching she put this into practice both for herself as a business owner, and for clients, coaching women through challenging supported journeys of their own selection. She also works in large organisations, coaching managers to improve performance faster.

As with many woman today who seek "fitness" for success and winning, Claudia has a long-standing involvement in fighting inequality.

She enjoys music, dancing, theatre, film, keeping fit, and reading the likes of Stephen Covey, Alice Walker and Toni Morrison. She is an experienced independent traveller, seeking open minds and open spaces. She supports the Centre for Women and Democracy, the Fawcett Society, National Deaf Children's Society, and Centrepoint.

She has an MBA, a Practitioner Coach Diploma (DipNMC), is an NLP Master Practitioner and an International Institute of Coaching member. She recognises that qualifications are also a part of the perseverance journey…to winning.

To win we must persevere but perseverance is not a long race— it's many, many short races. The question is how do we get fit to persevere and win?

Not long ago, working as the learning and development manager in a national organisation, the head of HR told me in two words that my world had ended: "You're redundant." Up to then, I was a conventional professional: recognised, with an identity through my work, active in equality matters, and with an MBA—"successful" and "winning" you could say. And at a personal level too: I was post-marriage and enjoying being single again, an independent world traveller, having lived solo in Brazil for a year. However, as I considered my last years of employment, disengaged and unchallenged was how I'd felt.

So, however subtly, I'd already been thinking of starting again. Two months after leaving my employers, I set up Winning Pathways Coaching, making a business of my long-standing commitment to enabling greater empowerment for women. Two years on, with a thriving coaching business and a burgeoning network marketing business, I realised that "winning" was as much fast-handling losing as glad-handing risk: an inviting, scary narrative, which always poses awkward questions about you and your journey towards what you want. Have you the nerve and commitment to get there? Let's find out from this work.

I'm a director, life coach, and colour coach at Winning Pathways Coaching. I work, mainly—though not exclusively—with women, to empower them. I'm also an independent consultant with Arbonne, a network marketing business in the health and wellness industry, which provides business opportunities for people and coaches them to succeed. All my work is informed by an active commitment to equality and overcoming barriers to full living. Does this seem a weird combination of businesses? Maybe, but this portfolio of work is quite common. My two businesses are united by two themes: coaching and empowering women to be more than they currently are.

What's this work about and why read it?

It's about three things:

- The nature of success and winning
- How four women have characterised winning

- How you can win—the five pillars to support your efforts and get you there faster

Why consider winning in life and work?

Writing this chapter, I wanted to give air time to some women we can learn from, "ordinary" women like you and me quietly creating extraordinary lives for themselves. So what's "ordinary"? I'm thinking of women who are not currently well known outside their professional fields. You may not have heard of them yet, but they are courageous, focused, making a difference in the lives of others, and transforming their own lives for the better—in other words, winning.

This chapter is a success narrative about the jagged journey towards winning of four empowered women: Bianca Forbes, Claire Brummell, Sarah Dunning, and Sherry Malik. All, like you and me, have experienced the challenges typical of women's lives—losses, broken relationships, lack of confidence, and more. What they have in common is that they have overcome these challenges and the ambiguities of success and have emerged as winners, and have helped others to be winners too. Let's learn from them.

The following section contains biographies of the four winning women and their journeys to winning in their own words.

Winning Woman 1

Bianca Forbes: The elder of two sisters, Bianca's childhood was atypical of black British families. Born in London, Bianca was blessed with a nonconformist mother, who joined the Hare Krishna movement and taught her daughters the value of going against the grain. Spending part of her childhood at a Hare Krishna boarding school in Worcestershire exposed Bianca to spirituality early on and shaped her resolve to always be there for her children. She is married with three children, and being there for them is at the root of what she does.

This is what Bianca says about her journey.

"It was an emotional journey that influenced what I'm doing now. When I was eight months pregnant with my daughter, my grandmother died. She was my second mum. I held back my grief because I didn't want my daughter to be affected. Then about year later my mom died. It was like all my people were leaving, and I was being punished for something.

I felt suicidal. This positive mindset that I'd had up until these losses didn't make sense. By that time, I'd started to have my children, and I knew I couldn't let them go through the experience I'd had in losing my mum—I had to stick around for them. So I got more involved with my passion to help people deal with their personal issues.

Getting up again and staying determined to achieve what I wanted to do was challenging. I did it through counselling, therapy, keeping journals, practicing a lot of self-help techniques and continuing to dream of having a business. I attended business training, got qualified, and got deeper in the personal development field, which kept me motivated, while helping other people and bringing all my new expertise together."

Bianca Forbes Ltd ("helping mums run their family and their business instead of having their family and their business run them") coaches mums to set up successful businesses and simultaneously be there for their children in a way that doesn't involve them compromising the two roles.

Winning Woman 2

Claire Brummell: Claire's positive, engaging, and inspiring personality belies the masculine mask she hid behind for more than twenty years. Claire was born and brought up in Kent, the older of two girls, by her mum an accounts manager and her dad, an IT project manager. Here's the story of her journey to winning in life and work.

"As a child, I was bullied by girls at every school I attended; therefore, I believed that women were bitchy, mean, and untrustworthy. I surrounded myself with male friends, becoming one of the boys to fit in…walking, talking, even dressing like them!

At university I studied IT. I was surrounded by guys, and I knew exactly how to be accepted; I played on their terms. I began my career in IT and then video games, both very masculine and competitive environments. I had to prove myself by being better than the guys around me to be thought just as good.

I transitioned into television, managing relationships, which I absolutely loved.

But when my team was moved to a new department, I realised how competitive the company was; it was 'get to the top at all costs, no matter what you do or who you tread on'. I was miserable and knew I'd never be successful there because that wasn't who I was. The little inner voice saying, 'You're not happy, you're not where you're supposed to be,' was getting louder.

I knew drastic change was required to work out the right direction for me. So at the beginning of the recession with no new job to transition to, I quit my job, my flat, and my lifestyle, and moved back in with family. Everyone thought I was crazy.

I got another job and thought I was heading in a better direction. What fascinates me is that when you think you're going in the right direction, but deep down you know you're not, life has a habit of jumping in and forcing change….often in a very dramatic way. At an event in London, I was trampled. I got rushed to hospital with back and neck injuries and was in bed for weeks.

It was a real low point…but also my turning point. As a result of my injuries I attended an event in Australia where I learnt about the concepts of 'masculinity and femininity.' I realised that I'd spent the last twenty years trying to be a guy—no wonder I'd been miserable! This opened me up to a whole new world, and I became an absolute sponge for information. Reconnecting with my femininity was having such a profound effect on me that I wanted to learn as much about it as I could.

I realised that information on femininity wasn't really accessible to 'real women' like me…so it became my mission to share it in a new and fun way. Reconnecting with my feminine essence has transformed my life. I'm happier, I feel more fulfilled, relaxed…like me again, and I wanted to give that gift to other women. So 'Feminine 1st' was born."

Claire coaches, speaks and runs workshops for women worldwide to help transform their lives by rediscovering and reconnecting with what is really important to them. She helps women to recognise the power of embracing their femininity while still being true to themselves; to understand and discover the balance of masculine and feminine that is right for them; to release the struggle for control and perfection that many experience. She gives them the tools to live the life they truly desire and deserve.

Winning Woman 3.

Sarah Dunning: Watching Sarah's engrossing presentation before a large audience, you'd never believe that three years ago she was a professional dancer, but shy and lacking in confidence. Sarah and her older brother were born and brought up in West Yorkshire. Her mom had her own hairdressing business and her dad was a regional manager in retail.

Dancing was Sarah's great love. She trained as a professional dancer at dance college in Blackpool. In 2008, she suffered a serious injury while performing on stage and was told to stop or else....she therefore swapped the instability and insecurity of professional dancing for the stability of teaching dance at The BRIT School. Bidding goodbye to her dearest love was tough, but with hindsight, she recognizes the alternative—a constant cycle of work, rejections, no job, and little money. But Sarah was crafting greater choices.

In May 2008, feeling lost and wondering what to do with her life, Sarah discovered *The Secret*[1] and *The Law of Attraction*[2] and asked for what she wanted. "I remember standing on my friend's balcony saying, 'I just want to do this.' It sounds really cheesy, but...I thought, 'I just want to do something that actually makes a difference to people.' Then literally a week later, I was told about this business opportunity, Arbonne, descibed as health and wellness products. I had no interest in that, but I've learnt a lesson—to be open minded. You shouldn't prejudge something that you think isn't for you, because you just never know. It was exactly what I was looking for, just in a different box."

Having excelled at dancing, Sarah gradually excelled in Arbonne, using the same characteristics of determination, tenacity, and discipline that had bolstered her as a performer. She developed a daily self-development routine using techniques such as affirmations,

---

[1] Rhonda Byrne, The Secret
[2] Rhonda Byrne, The Power

listening to motivational MP3s, and reading the likes of Brian Tracy and Robert Kiyosaki. She modelled herself on Arbonne superstars, and supported by coaching, Sarah's confidence and self-belief grew.

Now the first woman Arbonne National Vice President in England and highly respected and recognised by her peers, Sarah retired from the BRIT School earlier this year at the age of thirty-one and runs her Arbonne business full-time.

Winning Woman 4

Sherry Malik: The younger of two children, Sherry was born and brought up in India by her father, a civil servant, and her mother, a committed home maker. She is one of few minority ethnic women to have made it to the top of the social work profession.

Here she shares the story of her journey to winning in life and work.

"I left India and moved to California (via London) for six years, and then returned to London. So I'd lived on three continents by the time I was twenty-two, had two children in a strange country where I knew nobody, and had to make friends from scratch. My husband, a workaholic, wasn't around much, so I felt like a single parent. I went through a huge amount, living within a very unhappy marriage for twenty odd years, and then the death of my parents in a car accident fourteen years ago, which precipitated my divorce. All those things have been life changing, because you begin to evaluate what you want from life, what's important, and what isn't.

I used to live constantly in the future, because I couldn't bear the present. Life has taught me to become resilient, and to know that whatever it is you're going through, it won't last forever. You'll overcome it, ultimately there'll be a resolution, and it will be okay. Whatever I'm going through, I always ask myself, 'what's the worst that can happen?' Then when you really think of the worst that may occur, I ask myself, can I live with it? And I've never yet thought, 'no, I cannot."

Sherry's professional life began in nursery teaching but changed direction when she demonstrated her flair for leadership and social work that brought her sponsorship for social work training. As a trainee social worker, she began to appreciate the power of people empowerment, which has remained one of her values.

Throughout her twenty-six years in social work, Sherry has chosen appointments in social care organisations that, as Sherry put it, "are making a difference in the bigger sense." And as a senior manager, she has held steadfastly on to this value in organisations such as Action for Children, The Audit Commission, and Cafcass. She is currently chair of Essex Cares and Deputy Chief Executive of the soon to close, "General Social Care Council"[3] (GSCC). Her next planned move is to a chief executive post.

What's "Winning" in Life and Work?

"Winning" means different things to different people. Its synonyms fall in two groups;

- "Winning" as in appealing (engaging, attractive).
- "Winning" as in successful (triumphant, victorious).

The name *Winning Pathways Coaching* denotes success, but with a recognition that readers would ascribe their own meaning to it.

Commonly we relate success to financial wealth. Yet many wealthy people are miserable. Thousands of people are seeking the holy grail of financial success but, as we know, by itself money doesn't bring fulfillment .

We also relate success to celebrity status in a celebrity-obsessed world, fuelled by the media focus on famous women in particular, not for their talents, but for their appearance.

Success often appears easy to on-lookers who don't see the discipline, hard graft, frustration, and tears that characterise the winning process. It often starts to emerge in crises as it did with our participants.

Each participant here gave "winning," their own meaning, and neither money nor fame featured as primary motivators.

Bianca: Winning is "for you to actually be enjoying what your work is doing for your life. It's about succeeding and achieving."

---

[3] GSCC: The regulatory body for social workers

Claire*:* "Winning is knowing that I'm contributing, that I'm doing something to help other people, especially other women; that's why I set up my business. For me, winning in life is about fulfillment and having a great balance between my work and the life I want. My relationships are important. It's all about having quality time to spend with people who mean the most to me."

Sarah: "Winning in life and work, is a feeling of recognition from others in relation to what they identify as success, and gaining that success by working with integrity and honesty and having everyone's greatest interest at heart."

Sherry*:* "Winning is being at ease with myself; enjoying what I'm doing and coming away every day with a sense that I've moved forward, learned something new, had a good day, and that I've had a chance to contribute and change something for the better…It's about contentment"

The meaning each of them gave to "winning" aligned with their values.[4] Contributing and making a difference to other people's lives is inherent in "winning" for all—in other words, doing something worthwhile and fulfilling. They all regard "winning" as being about having choices and taking responsibility for winning, rather than leaving it to chance.

Five Pillars for Women to Win in Life and Work
Pillar 1: Know Who You Are.
Identify What Winning in Life and Work Means to You

Winning is personal; it's whatever it represents to you. Your gender, background, experiences, memories, beliefs, and values together determine your uniqueness. You are a woman with many roles: wife, mother, friend, business owner, employee, manager. What are your expectations of yourself within these roles? How do they compare with expectations from others, along with race and gender stereotypes? Some of us buy into the media constructs of women as

---

[4] Values are our highest priorities and deeply held drivers. They determine our actions

Madonnas, whores, or superwomen. If you don't know who you are as a woman, there's a danger that you'll be who you are told to be.

So bearing in mind the power of who you are, what does winning in life and work mean for you in the context of your various roles and your expectations of yourself within them? Avoid getting boxed in by gender stereotypes. You can be and do whatever you want regardless of gender and ethnicity. To answer this, consider what your life and work would be like if you were winning. Your values will be inherent.

Clarify Your Values

Clarifying one's values "is a way to create a map that will guide (you) them along the decision paths of (your) their lives."[5] Here's a technique to help you clarify your values as we're not always aware of them. Elicit them by identifying what's important to you in the context of life and then what's important to you in the work context. Elicit your values for each group separately.

- List all the words that come up until your list is complete.
- Compare the words on your list. Ask, "which is most important, this or that?" Place them in order of importance in terms of how they've shown up in your life until now. Be honest and you'll get some insight into why your life has turned out this way. You may dislike your findings, but you can consciously change your life's path by changing the importance you attach to each value.
- Return to the question of how your life and work would be if you were winning in the context of your values. This will show you what is really essential for you to win in work and life.

When you know what winning in life and work mean for you, you're on the road to embracing who you are. Consciously grasping the meaning of winning for *you* highlights how you have chosen to create yourself and gives immense clarity.

---

[5] Kimsey-House, Kimsey-House, Whitworth, and Sandhal: Co-Active Coaching

Claire: "In the corporate world, people would have called me 'a success,' or say I was 'winning in work,' because I was doing well at a job and earning a lot, but that wasn't 'winning' for me. I knew I could give more. What lights me up is helping others. The work I was doing wasn't something I could say, 'This is making a great difference in the world or to somebody's life,' and making a difference is really valuable to me."

Pillar 2: Know What You Want.

Seek Your Passion and Purpose

Great winners such as Marie Curie and Mother Theresa were driven by a passion for their craft or the outcome of exploiting that craft. Passion or your great love creates energy and motivation; it's what reinvigorates you when things get tough. Without passion your endeavours are likely to topple. You may drive a Ferrari or inhabit a mansion, but without passion you won't be happy. As women we're supposed to love shopping, shoes, being wives and mothers. These are powerful stereotypes. Love what *you* love, whatever that is, not what you're expected to love.

Sarah is driven by improving life for others.

"I've gained respect from lots of people that I respect, and that's enabled me to have a voice, which gives you a certain amount of power to improve things for others; and if you work with integrity, and I know that I do, I know I can improve things for everyone else."

Bianca is driven by business and motherhood. She has combined the two in her business.

I'm passionate about "being there for my children, growing with them from spiritual and personal development perspectives...Bianca Forbes Ltd helps mums to be there for their children and have a successful business in a way that doesn't make them have to choose between the two."

Passion may not just be about "heart space."[6] It might not be an emotional and warm thing. It could be about "head space,"[7]

---

[6] Dr Joanna Martin , director, "Shift Speaker Training"
[7] Dr Joanna Martin, director, "Shift Speaker Training"

something that fascinates you intellectually; for example, some people are fascinated by problem solving. So ask yourself:

- What really turns me on?
- What do I think and talk about a lot of the time?
- What fascinates me so much that it's hard to distract me from it?
- What could I talk about without getting bored?

List the key words in each of your answers: it's likely they are the same words.

Finding your passion will guide you into what you need to do to win. But passion alone is insufficient. Life has to be meaningful for us to thrive and feel content. And meaning comes with a sense of purpose, in other words, the reason for which you feel you are in the world, your "This is it!"[8] When people are unable to identify their "This is it!" feeling, no matter how successful they are at work or in relationships, their life will lack meaning and a sense of fulfillment. You can spot people with a sense of purpose—they are likely to be:

- Focused on others rather than on themselves.

Sherry: "When I was younger, 'winning' was more about myself. Now that I'm older, winning is about other people. It's not just about me anymore."

- Contributing and making a difference

Sarah's business offers a business opportunity. She says:
"I've seen Arbonne change people's lives, and it's just like giving someone hope that they can achieve things that they almost shelved and thought aren't possible any more."

- Serving a cause greater than themselves.

Claire: "I got feedback from people I was working with saying, 'this is really making a difference to me.' When I helped somebody

---

[8] Julia Hastings, You're Great!

completely transform their life…realising what they wanted and that there was nothing stopping them from having it, I thought, 'Wow! This is what lights me up and makes me feel fulfilled.' At my first speaking engagement somebody asked, 'Were you nervous?' I said, 'Well, I had butterflies before I got up there. But as soon as I was out there sharing my story, which I could see was of value to women in the audience, I just knew—this is where I'm supposed to be. This is what I'm supposed to be doing."

Your purpose doesn't have to be grand or reflect media or cultural stereotypes of women. When attached to your values and passion your purpose will be particular to who you are.

Often it takes a crisis, tragedy, or a bereavement to discover one's purpose. Claire and Sarah suffered serious injuries in accidents, which started a chain of events that resulted in the discovery of their sense of purpose. Both went on to set up their businesses. Bianca's bereavements and grieving uncovered her sense of purpose as well.

But crises are not necessary to gain your sense of purpose. You can consciously do so whenever you choose. So how do you discover your purpose? The following questions will guide you. Quickly jot down the first answer to each question that comes to mind.

1. What do you love to do?
2. What absorbs your attention so that you lose track of time?
3. What makes you feel fantastic about yourself?
4. Who inspires you more than anyone else and why?
5. What are you naturally good at?
6. What do people compliment you on?
7. If you knew you couldn't fail, what would you do?
8. What are your top five values?
9. What causes do you strongly believe in?
10. How could you use your talent, values, and passion to contribute to other people, organisations, or causes?

Now that you know your passion and your purpose, you will sense some direction to your life. The next step is to write your personal mission statement, **which "focuses on what you want to be (character) and to do (contributions and achievements) and on**

the values or principles upon which being and doing are based.'"[9]
Take time over it and listen to your heart. You'll know what you
want in life. This might change as you change over time, but for
now you'll know your winning pathway.

All four winning women are making a contribution through
what they do.

Sherry: 'When I was a nursery school teacher in America, I
was more interested in what was going on in the family than I was in
the classroom. The kids would play up and I was more interested in
resolving some of that. When I moved permanently to this country, I
started managing a day nursery for homeless families in Barnet.
Within a year I'd expanded the provision and done loads of other
things that weren't part of my remit. The director spotted me and
said, 'would you like to train to be a social worker? We'll pay your
fees and salary.' I got into social work from there, because that was
absolutely my thing."

Bianca: "When I did my research, the moms rather than the dads
were the ones talking about their challenges of juggling family and
work and about being overwhelmed and unsupported. It just made
sense for me to focus on this one business because I'd experienced
what they were talking about; it was a natural progression."

Pillar 3: Know Where You're Going.

Create Your Vision:

The most common characteristic of leaders at all levels is vision."[10]
Having a vision realises possibilities and awakens insight,
resourcefulness, and action. It provides direction and enables
visualisation of where you want to go. If you can imagine it, you can
move from here to there swiftly. "Creative visualisation is the art of
using your imagination to create what you want in your life."[11]
President Kennedy had a vision of putting a man on the moon. It
seemed impossible at the time, but it became a reality. Such is the

---

[9] Stephen R. Covey, The 7 Habits of Highly Effective People
[10] Brian Tracy Goals!
[11] Julia Hastings, You Can Have What You Want

power of vision. "Whatever the mind of man can conceive and believe, it can achieve."[12]

So create your vision of winning in life and work as it relates to your passion and purpose and visualise it daily. Make the images powerful and compelling; add bright colours and high-volme sounds. See what you're doing. Feel how it feels. Hear the sounds around you. Then start the process of making your vision a reality.

Set Your Goals:

Winning women are goal oriented. Goals give focus, direction, and single-mindedness. Clear-cut goals boost your confidence and increase your drive. "Without goals you simply drift and flow on the currents of life. With goals you fly like an arrow straight and true to your target."[13]

Set your goals using this technique. Write down what you want as it relates to winning in life and work using the CREATE model, i.e. concise and clear, realistic, ecological (safe for you, others, and the planet), written as if now, (in the present tense and positive), time-bounded, with an end-step (something that tells you that you've won). For example: It is 31.12.12, I'm chief executive officer in a children's social care organisation. I'm sitting in a meeting with my directors, sharing my vision for the organisation.

Place your goal where you can read it every day.

Sarah used visualisation to help her scale the different levels in Arbonne and she and her team set monthly goals to move toward their targets.

Develop Your Action Plan:

A goal without an action plan will get you nowhere. "Your ability to set goals and make plans for their accomplishment is the "master skill" of success."[14] Action planning with clear deadlines enables you to identify specific steps to take to achieve your goals. It makes you

---

[12] Napoleon Hill, Think and Grow Rich
[13] Brian Tracy, Goals!
[14] Brian Tracy, Goals!

- proactive rather than reactive
- identify the main elements to address for success, likely obstacles and solutions
- spot strengths, opportunities, and support
- focus

It is this process of thinking through the planning that's significant, rather than the plan itself. So sit down with a sheet of paper and get planning. Sometimes stuff happens unexpectedly and you have to change your plan, but that's okay; the important thing is that you have a plan.

All our winning women have a clear vision of where they are going, with goals and action plans to make it happen.

Sherry: "When I was twenty-seven, I was taking this course in which I had to write down my five-year plan. When I was moving six years later, I found these papers with that five-year plan, and I was gobsmacked, because I had achieved every single thing. Since then I have always had a five-year plan.''

Pillar 4: Know How to Get There.

So you have your goal and action plan—it's implementation time. You're working to make it happen, putting in time and effort each day, perhaps alongside your regular employment and caring for your children. Initially, you're on a high. With regular visualisation your vision remains clear. Then gradually, it may start to feel like hard work. You realise that winning doesn't happen overnight and you start to feel jaded. Challenges emerge—life crises, demands from your children or partner, naysayers or well-meaning people who don't understand what you're doing and try to dissuade you, plans that fall through, mistakes made, guilt for going for what you want (women are good at that!), or you might simply lack knowledge or skills to get what you want. Challenges try us, keep us alert. They exploit our cache of courage, tenacity, and resilience, characteristics we may have taken for granted.

Overcome Challenges

So how do you overcome such challenges? All our winning women were tested on the way to winning and beat their challenges in their own particular ways.

Sarah: "I felt at the time that every single person in my life was telling me not to do it. I had to be really focused to keep going."

Sherry: "The main challenges were my divorce and the death of my parents, which more or less coincided. They developed my resilience, giving me a perspective on life, and I thought, 'You just have to live for each day, so enjoy every moment.'"

Claire: "I've been going through a break-up of a relationship recently and found that being somebody who people look up to can sometimes be challenging. It's not easy to lay yourself bare and say, 'I'm perfectly imperfect,' I'm human, and I have challenges too."

Bianca: "When I suffered all those losses, getting back up again and staying determined to do what I wanted to do...I practiced a lot of self-help techniques and holding on to my dream."

It's easy to see challenges as obstacles to our attempts to win. But when you embrace and reframe them, regard them optimistically as opportunities for learning, your attitude becomes more constructive. Approach challenges with curiosity, asking, "How can I learn and benefit from this?" Then apply that learning to ensure that you benefit, regardless of the nature of the challenge.

Put Yourself First:

Women are programmed to be caretakers and have difficulty prioritising their own needs. Put yourself at the top of your priority list and get your needs met. You'll be up-beat and energised, better able to meet the needs of your family.

Seek Help and Support:

We often buy into the media construct of having to be superwomen and have difficulty seeking help or support. On the journey, delegate tasks to others who have skills that you need and don't have. Be clear about the type of support you need and create and draw on your support network of people willing to back you.

Get a Coach or a Mentor:

Coaching and mentoring are powerful action-focused ways to get what you want, which is why superstars, whatever their field, all have coaches or mentors. The difference is that mentoring is usually undertaken by someone in your field, who can share their knowledge and advise you. A coach doesn't need to have a background in your field, because they neither advise nor tell you what to do. They help you find the answers for yourself.

So how will coaching/mentoring benefit you? First, it moves you from here to where you want to go faster than travelling solo. It helps you to overcome those negative emotions (e.g. fear), negative self-talk, (e.g. "You can't do this"), and limiting beliefs, (e.g. "I'm not good enough"), that hamper your success. It increases your personal power so that you're in control. In other words, coaching/mentoring can transform your life. With a coach/mentor alongside you, working to your agenda, guiding, supporting, and encouraging you, while holding you accountable, you're more likely to win.

Our winning women have all benefited from coaching or mentoring.

Bianca: "Coaches have been great to cheer me on. They've helped me by not letting me off the hook when I've slipped into self-doubt. It makes the world of difference to have someone totally committed to your cause."

Sherry: "As for mentoring/coaching, my philosophy is to talk to many different people for the different issues I'm facing. The temptation is to withdraw and do it by yourself, but it's always a better outcome if you can use friends, colleagues, or a mentor/coach to sound out different concerns."

Sarah's mentor gave her: "A vision for what this business is going to be in the future, along with support and encouragement, and was just able to raise the bar higher than I thought it could be."

Claire: "I would probably say that Tony Robbins was my biggest mentor...it was at a seminar of his that I first learned about masculinity and femininity, and that gave me the inspiration to start my business."

Be a "Go-Giver"[15]:

Our winning women are "go-getters"—they make things happen. And their values and definition of winning are tied to contributing, which makes them "go-givers" as well. Go-givers are people-focused rather than self-focused. They add value[16] to others and thereby help those people considerably while enhancing their own sense of pleasure and improving their business and personal outcomes. When you add real value to other people's lives, whether on a personal or business level, they'll feel good about you and add value to your life too. And imagine what that will add to your journey towards winning? So take a "How can I add value to others?" approach to your efforts to win.

Be Open to Inspiration:

Draw on those who inspire you. They could be your parents, friends, entrepreneurs, or maybe people you meet at random whose actions stir you in some way. Learn from them and apply the learning to your daily activities.

Claire: "I am blessed that I get inspired by people around me all the time. I can see inspiration in so many different things at so many different levels that I'm constantly being inspired."

Sherry: "People inspire me every day. It doesn't matter who they are; everyone's got something to offer. So I seek my inspiration from everybody. I notice when people are good at things, and I say, 'You do that so well; how do you do it?'"

Bianca: "My mum was very inspirational in terms of practicality and what it means to be a mum and being open and honest."

Sarah: "One of my real inspirations is my dad. He's fabulous—positive and filled with gratitude. I've learned his strength and directness combined with integrity, consideration for other people, and love. My mum too gives unconditional love. And my teacher Pamela Grey, who pushed me to work at a level that I never thought possible."

---

[15] Bob Burg and John David Mann, Go-Givers Sell More
[16] Value is the relative worth or desirability of a thing or experience to the user (Burg and Mann).

Put in Time and Effort:

You cannot win by sitting back and talking about it. Activity is essential. Winners do more than non-winners: they put in time and effort and get results.

Claire: "When I started the company, I was still working full-time. I would start at 5 a.m. and work until midnight, so that I could work on the business around the other job I was doing."

Sherry: "Someone put a recommendation about me on LinkedIn, unsolicited, saying that I'd enabled some of their best work in a closing organisation (The GSCC). They were really pleased because it's so easy to give up when you're closing down."

Sarah: "I was in school by 7.00 a.m. and leave at 6 p.m. the earliest, then go straight to work at my Arbonne business until midnight. I did that for about a year."

Pillar 5: Know You Can Do It.

Believe in yourself:

Self-belief is confidence in your own abilities or judgements and is vital to winning. Lack of self-belief sabotages your efforts on the journey to winning. Whatever you believe about yourself, that's what you'll be. "Whether you think that you can, or that you can't, you're usually right."[17] How many things have you not done because you thought, "I can't"?

When we hold limiting beliefs about what we can achieve, then through our unconscious mind we automatically limit our actions and the results. Telling yourself you'll fail becomes self-fulfilling. So when challenges appear, you won't go the extra mile to overcome them.

Here's the good news: change your mindset and you can develop unshakeable self-belief and confidence. Your unconscious mind is a warehouse of all your experiences, memories, skills, values, and beliefs. Through repetition of behaviour and thoughts, it's programmed to respond in certain ways. For example, with regular practice of a new skill such as driving, eventually you can drive

---

[17] Quote from Henry Ford

without thinking about it. It's the same with self-belief. If you were told regularly as a young girl that you weren't good at math, that's what you continue to believe in adulthood, and that's how you'll perform in relation to numbers. However, change your mindset about this by reprogramming your unconscious, and you'll believe differently and get a different outcome. So to reprogram your unconscious and develop self belief:

- Accept that *you* control your thoughts, your actions, and your outcomes. Remember, *you*, not destiny nor anyone else, are in charge of your life.
- Visualise achieving your goals and the steps you're taking to get there.
- Develop positive affirmations[18] about you and your abilities, and repeat them with conviction regularly each day. For example, "I am a winner!" or "I am an effective chief executive in a children's service," or "I am an effective, caring mom."

Develop Yourself:

There are a number of means to develop yourself, which our winning women utilised.

- Find your role models: identify those who've made a similar journey, who share your top values and inspire you. Follow their example. Why reinvent the wheel when you can learn from others? Sarah modeled herself on her sponsor and other Arbonne leading lights, believing that if their system worked for them it would work for her—and it did.
- Identify skills you need to achieve your goals and invest in yourself by attending courses, seminars, workshops and reading relevant literature. Bianca did business study, which equipped her to set up her businesses. Claire trained with Anthony Robbins. Sherry took

---

[18] Affirmations: positive statements regarding a desired situation, repeated regularly to trigger the unconscious into positive action. To be effective, affirmations should be repeated with conviction.

advantage of the offer of funding for social work training. Sarah read and read and utilised Arbonne's training to develop her business skills.

And Finally...

Winning in life and work is whatever it means to you as a woman. It relates to the five pillars. Know:

- Who you are
- What you want,
- Where you're going
- How to get there
- You can do it

So now you know what the five pillars include, get going; do what you need to do to win. Remember, winning doesn't happen overnight. You'll encounter challenges along the way, which you can surmount and come out stronger. Commit yourself to winning; stay focused; be patient; use your supporters and your coach or mentor. And you'll get there—you will win.

Here's some advice from our winning women.

Bianca: "Stick to your values. That's what will make you stand your ground and stand out. It will empower you to go against the grain and do things differently."

Claire: "If you're seeking your life's purpose, start looking inside; listen to your heart and what's important to you. Your purpose doesn't have to be to change the world. It could be to be an inspiring mum. It's about embracing what's really important to you and celebrating that, no matter how big or small it seems."

Sarah: "Love what you're doing and don't do something just for money."

Sherry: "Be authentic or you'll get exposed. Find your passion. I remember thinking, 'If I start doing this, I'll be stuck in it.' Well, you don't have to do it for the rest of your life. If you don't discover your passion there, move on."

The Secret Ingredient to Winning in Life and Work

by John Brant

John Brant is a speaker, trainer, and coach helping people and businesses turbo boost their sales, leadership, and relationship building skills. John has helped start-up businesses grow from no clients to fully franchised, and has helped many other professionals to break free from fears holding them back. In addition to his business activities, John is also an investor and owns a personal property portfolio.

As a former actuarial consultant, John helped to advise the boards of some of the UK's top FTSE 100 companies on their pensions and investment strategy and was responsible for developing and enhancing key client relationships.

John regularly takes time out to travel the world and has spent time in places as far and wide as Vietnam, Thailand, the East and West Coast of Australia, New Zealand, India, South Africa, Tahiti, Canada, the USA, Eastern Europe, Nepal and South America. To find out more about John, check out his profile on LinkedIn.

If you want to win in life and work and have so far come up short, you may be missing the magical secret ingredient. This chapter will reveal and discuss the fundamental elements of the secret ingredient. I will share stories relating to some of the discoveries I have made along my journey relating to this secret and some tips for locating and looking after it once you find it. You will also find some exercises to help you build a winning vision for your life and work.

I once had a business with a network or multilevel marketing company. The training was great, the people were great—it really was a great business in a box. Only one problem: my business was failing. We were told to focus on following the system and increasing our activity, then results would follow. It was a numbers game: if your conversion rates were only half as good as the next guy, approach twice as many people! Perhaps you can relate to the "work harder" strategy and the "follow the system" strategy for success? However, not everyone who has worked hard and followed the business system has become successful. There is a magical, secret ingredient that I now recognise was missing from my business. In fact, in my experience, success is very hard to come by until you have developed this secret ingredient.

As I continued to study success and what it is that really makes a difference in work and life, I started to see this secret ingredient in every great leader. I saw it in great comedians, great sportsmen, and great businessmen. This ingredient is secret because it's not something you can see, hear, or touch directly, and it's certainly not something that the business books will tell you much about. To some this secret ingredient is mysterious and difficult to define. The people who have it usually rise to the top quickly. People want to listen to them and they are naturally persuasive and influential. They light up a room with their presence and inspire others to higher and greater achievements. They sail smoothly over the choppiest of waters and find unbounded energy for overcoming any obstacles placed in their path. They create win/win outcomes and are often universally admired and even loved. ***What is this mysterious, secret ingredient?***

Before I reveal the secret ingredient, I need to first discuss a matter of philosophy. The biggest difference between those who know this secret ingredient and those who don't is a *Be-Do-Have* philosophy. There is a story I heard once about three brothers given away at birth by a mother who was incapable of looking after them due to illness. The first boy went to a family where a fancy lifestyle was valued most, the second boy went to a family where hard work was valued most, and the third boy went to a family where good character was valued most. It turned out after many years that the mother recovered from her illness and she set out to discover how well her boys were doing in life. The first boy she found was from the family where a fancy lifestyle was valued most. The journey was long and arduous and the roads were so bumpy that she never got the opportunity to enjoy the view. After an emotional reunion, she asked her boy about whether he had achieved happiness. The first boy shared that he still had some way to go to be happy. He was working hard, and he would be happy once he got to live in the house he wanted and drove the car of his choice. The burden of his debt was, however, weighing down heavily upon him right now. Her second boy was hard to get hold of. He never returned her calls and was always at work. When she finally got to meet him, all was not well: he wasn't sleeping well and his wife was complaining all the time. She discovered that he too still had some way to go to be happy. He insisted that his hard work would pay off soon and he would then be able to spend time with the people he loved. Her third boy greeted his mother with open arms. His eyes sparkled, he was well spoken, and he made her feel especially welcome. He shared with his mother all the exciting things that had happened to him since she had last seen him. He described how his new family encouraged him to become the person he needed to be so that he could do and have whatever he wanted. There was only one question he had been taught to focus on: Who must I become to have the life I want? He confirmed he was happy, and success followed him wherever he went.

Let me share with you the *Have-Do-Be* trap that I have seen many people fall into. Most people live by the philosophy that once I *have* the money, I can *do* what I want, and then I'll *be* happy. The truth is, you can never be happy except in the present moment, and those in the *have-do-be* trap put off happiness until some future date (which of course may never come). I also hear some people live by the philosophy that once I *have* someone else's approval, I can *do* what I need to do, and then I can *be* successful. In my experience, the only recipe for long-term success and empowerment from day one is the *Be-Do-Have* formula. If you want happiness, you must decide to *be* a happy person first, and find something you are happy to be *do*ing. Only then will you be willing to *do* the things you need to *do* for long enough until you *have* what you want. If you want success, first and foremost you must decide to *be* the type of person that creates success. Once you are that person, you will *do* what is required: only then will you *have* the results you are looking for.

The secret ingredient I have been referring to is the secret of *charisma*. For many people, charisma is hard to define but easy to spot. The term "charisma" comes from a Greek word meaning "the gift of grace." For the purposes of this chapter, I take the definition of charisma to be "the ability to express and be yourself fully." The one thing that the leaders and successful people in my network marketing company had in common was that these people had charisma. There is no doubt that if you are someone who has charisma, you move onto the fast track. If you are charismatic, you are often the one who gets paid more.

I have come to observe that all of us are inherently charismatic, in fact, we are all born with charisma. You just have to observe how a young child won't hold themselves back when expressing themselves. Sometimes, however, we don't let our charisma shine through in all our dealings with people. If you are having difficulty believing right now that you have charisma, I want you to think about situations where you are very comfortable and you have a positive impact on others. That might be a social night with close friends, or time with your family. Now contrast that with how you communicate and act in perhaps more unfamiliar social situations, where nerves might take over. As a general rule, your charisma level drops in situations where fear shows up. Before developing the concepts and tips I am going to share with you, I was often uncomfortable when thrown into a social situation with my peer group. If anything similar happens nowadays, I have quick and easy techniques to tap back into a healthy sense of self, some of which I will be sharing with you in this chapter. Through my coaching and training programs, I now work with people to express themselves more effectively to break free of shyness, become stronger leaders, more effective sales people, and better at building relationships—all of which enables them to release their inherent charisma.

Introduction to the Secrets of Charismatic Communication

The secrets disclosed in this chapter have been distilled based upon:

- Study of the character and traits of charismatic leaders such as Nelson Mandela, Richard Branson, Mother Teresa, and Martin Luther King.
- Insights into the character of the most charismatic people I know.
- Work with my clients.
- My own personal experience in developing charisma.

The secrets you are about to discover can impact your life profoundly if they are embodied fully and worked on over a prolonged period. Although quantum leaps are possible, it will not serve you to do anything other than treat these secrets as a lifetime's work. I also subscribe fully to the philosophy that what matters is not where you are now but where you are heading. Leaders are those who put this philosophy into practice. In this chapter I provide some simple tools and exercises you can use to develop your charisma quickly. We will also consider the concept of living a charismatic life.

First let's take a deeper look at what philosophy charismatic people subscribe to. The key elements of this philosophy have been distilled into three areas:

- Self-expression
- Intention to be of Service
- Desire for Personal Mastery

A. Self-Expression

In nature, if we take a look around, we can see that if a plant or animal is not growing or adapting itself to its environment it will die. We also can see from the business world that companies or government revenues that are not growing are those that get into financial trouble. Expansion and multiplication are the ways of nature. Self-expression is the expansion of the self and is our natural state. Have you ever heard the phrase "I am dying inside"? This can only happen if we choose to stop expressing our natural or authentic selves and start conforming to what others want for us instead.

Discovery 1. What others think of you is none of your business!

One of the quickest ways of destroying self-expression is to worry about what others are thinking of you. This form of worry is destructive because you are working with pure speculation. This kind of thinking goes round and round in the mind, usually without much (if any) obvious benefit, draining your energy and your focus. It robs individuals of the assurance and presence they need to develop charisma (see below).

In practice, people spend most of the time thinking about themselves, not anyone else. In any case, whatever they are thinking or saying about you really expresses more about them than about you.

If you are in the habit of worrying what others think of you, check out the tips contained in the sections on courage, self-awareness, certainty, and presence.

There are three attributes linked to self-expression, which lie on the path to charisma. The three attributes are passion, meaning and certainty.

A1. Passion:
"The more intensely we feel about an idea or a goal, the more assuredly the idea, buried deep in our subconscious, will direct us along the path to its fulfillment."
—Earl Nightingale

There are two types of passion: passion of the mind and of the heart. The first part of my work life was driven by the passion of the mind. I loved the intellectual challenge of the actuarial profession in which I took part (actuaries look after the financial health of insurance companies and pension funds). Passion of the mind can also be called a passion for learning or for intellectual growth and discovery. The second passion is that of the heart. This passion is distinct from that of the mind, as it is not based upon intellect. You will recognise a passion of the heart when it is connected to a sense of a deeper meaning for you (e.g. inspiring others) rather than an intellectual triumph. There is one crucial difference between these two passions from the perspective of becoming a charismatic communicator. Passion of the mind does not lead directly to charisma, whereas passion of the heart does (note that there is one item up for debate, which is humour—often a blend of heart and mind and can be very charismatic). This is because passion of the mind does not tap into self-expression. Passion of the mind seeks to understand the world from an objective standpoint, whereas passion of the heart seeks self-expression, and it is self-expression that is intensely attractive to others.

Tip: If you want to start to develop your charisma and don't have passion for your work, consider how to create more meaning from what you do. Consider the wider benefits your company delivers and how your actions are making a difference in the world—don't underestimate the value you are helping to provide for the benefit of people's lives.

A2. Meaning.
"So many people walk around with a meaningless life. They seem half-asleep, even when they're busy doing things they think are important. This is because they're chasing the wrong things. The way you get meaning into your life is to devote yourself to loving others, devote yourself to your community around you, and devote yourself to creating something that gives you purpose and meaning."
—Morrie Schwartz

There are three stages of meaning. The first stage is the physical stage—things have meaning for you because of the physical pleasure they bring to you, or the pain that they help you to avoid. For example, this could be the sense of meaning you get from being physically intimate with your partner, from enjoying your favourite food, or from having a roof over your head. The second stage is what I call the business stage. This is the sense of meaning we get from the cycle of giving and receiving and is the stage that most business operates. Many people get immense meaning from the challenges and rewards of their career or business. The third stage is the freedom stage. This is the sense of meaning derived purely from being and the ability to exercise choice. This is the spiritual aspect of meaning and is the stage is characterised by gratitude, peace, and acceptance. Many people live most areas of their life at stage one of meaning. Although there is an element of Self-expression at stage one, without the context of stages two and three, many people get lost in the addictions associated with stage one, and life becomes a means to an end—they will only do something if it suits their "selfish" interest. Addictions in themselves close down natural self-expression almost by definition—for example, an alcoholic looking for their next drink has a severely restricted ability to self-express. Those communicating at level one of meaning tend to have a purpose linked to getting whatever they can get. They naturally believe that other people think the same way, as their awareness doesn't tend to expand beyond their own sources of pleasure and pain. Fear tends to manifest as their desires are based upon their needs only (e.g. they can worry that someone else may deny them something pleasurable).

Those with highly developed charisma tend to derive meaning from stages two and three. If someone is genuinely there to help you and has your best interests at heart, you can sense their commitment to this whether or not they expect something in return. The primary question charismatic leaders ask themselves is: "How can I add value?" and their purpose is linked to inspiring more from themselves and others. They recognise that there is something more important than at the level of their own physical desires.

Tip: To create more meaning in your life, practice being grateful and accepting of what you already have.

A3. Certainty and Assurance
"If a man will begin with certainties, he shall end in doubts: but if he will be content to begin with doubts, he shall end in certainties."
—Francis Bacon

The third foundation of charisma is the attractive air of certainty and assurance. This is evident in charismatic people when things are rosy, but it is most evident when they are assured under pressure.

What is clear for those with highly developed charisma is that they make their decisions in alignment with their principles and what they value most. These principles are internally driven and do not change, even under extreme pressure from others around them. Situations change but principles do not. This is why the charismatic person usually has immense self-belief and doesn't feel threatened when challenged. They are able to deal with far more uncertainty than the average person. As a result, they also don't see the need to control others.

The charismatic communicator also holds a simple vision. The simpler the vision, the more certainty is associated to it, and it is natural for them to be able to speak with more clarity than most. Charismatic people focus on what they know and can be certain about, and let go of things they can't know. States of personal certainty inspire states of certainty in others, which is why charisma is so closely linked to effective leadership.

Tip: Certainty is an emotional state. Practice going into a state of certainty by reliving (in your mind) a time in your past when you had strong feelings of certainty. The more you practice, the more you can go into this state any time you need it. Alternatively, you can set up a unique physical association while in this state (e.g. clicking your fingers when you are feeling most certain), and you can also create a trigger to access this state of certainty at any time.

Discovery 2. Letting Go...

One of the most charismatic leaders I have worked with is one of my old bosses when I worked in a large consultancy in London. I shall always remember his attitude when I handed in my resignation. My former boss's questioning was focused on understanding why I had made the decision, and he clearly had my best interests at heart. My decision was accepted graciously and with honour.

This is a trait of virtually all charismatic people I have met. They have an intention and expectation but never an attachment to a particular course of action. They think of the bigger picture and are keen that others choose a course of action that is right for them in the long run.

If you sometimes have the desire to control other people or need to let go of the view that people "should" be a particular way, or that you "have to" take a particular approach, I suggest you consider what internally driven principles you could adopt, and what externally driven principles you could relinquish.

B. Attributes of the Intention To Be of Service

Second of the three key philosophies associated with charisma is the intention to be of service. Common sense tells us that a person's intention is linked with outcome and end result. In my experience, the intention to serve others is the key to being perceived as charismatic.

Charismatic people that I have researched tend to recognise the interconnectedness of all things. They also implicitly (and sometimes explicitly) believe in karma, i.e. if you do good things for others, life will be good to you. Implicitly they are aware that there is something larger than themselves and their own wants and needs.

There are two attributes linked to the intention to be of service: connecting with others and being courageous.

B1. Connecting with others
"Whenever you're in conflict with someone, there is one factor that can make the difference between damaging your relationship and deepening it. That factor is attitude."
—William James

Connection can be a difficult thing to describe but an easy thing to recognise. Connecting with others at its simplest is liking them. The opposite of connecting is blame and attack, and we can only show this behaviour if we are in our minds, not in our hearts.

We have already discussed that charismatic communication comes from the heart, not the mind. When we are connected to our heart, we are also connected to the invisible intelligence (or wisdom) that is life itself. We can then connect to the natural flow—the same flow that allows oak trees to grow, seemingly without effect, from just a small acorn. When we are connected to our heart, we also become more connected with others. We can recognise that we are not independent beings. Note that the mind often leads us to think the opposite.

Tip: To connect more with others, become aware of when you may be blaming or attacking others. Instead put your attention into your heart, and the use the sights, sounds, and feelings from your natural senses to stay present.

B2. Courage
"Courage is the discovery that you may not win, and trying when you know you can lose." —Tom Krause

Fear is an attribute of the mind, and courage is the typical response for those who have developed charisma. The word "courage" originally comes from French and Latin indicating "of the heart." Charismatic communicators will typically trust their higher intuition and have trained themselves to remain connected to their heart during times of stress.

Charismatic people have developed the courage to be themselves, and believe in themselves even when others are doubting or don't agree with them.

Tip: Courage is a habit. Next time someone asks for a volunteer, be the first. Congratulate and reward yourself when you have built up the courage to do something of value, when you have feelings of discomfort or sense fear.

> **Discovery 3: Charismatic communication appeals to the emotions.**
>
> **Dr Martin Luther King Jr's famous "I have a dream" speech was given on August 28, 1963, and is widely recognised as one of the turning points for the civil rights movement in the United States of America.**
>
> **This speech was so successful because it captured both the hearts and minds of his followers. As well as being rich in metaphor and attractive language, this speech was designed to engender positive emotional states, including certainty and assurance as a result of a simple vision.**
>
> **Most people take action based upon emotion, so next time you want to persuade and influence, try putting people into empowering states by using positive emotion.**

C. Attributes of the Desire for Personal Mastery

Third of the key philosophies associated with charisma is the desire for personal mastery. Personal mastery leads to a sense of freedom and being able to act for the greater good, rather than reacting to circumstances based solely upon the restricted viewpoint of the mind and body.

There are two attributes linked to the desire for personal mastery: possession of presence and self-awareness.

C1. Presence
"As we are liberated from our own fear, our presence automatically liberates others." —Marianne Williamson

The mind is a wonderful tool and is capable of amazing intellectual feats. The abilities human beings have to understand and communicate concepts of great complexity to others set us apart from the animal kingdom.

Language and thinking has developed for us to enable us to communicate and generalise appropriately. In this chapter, "thought" is taken to mean internalised words or language—there is no "reality" inherent in the conceptual thought world on its own. The thought world and "reality" are in fact very different.

The average person has around 70,000 thoughts every single day, and thoughts take our attention away from a state of presence. The vast majority of thoughts take us directly into thinking about the past or thinking about the future, usually with the intention of avoiding pain or seeking pleasure. The thinking mind is therefore good for conceptual work, but it often creates agitation if left to its own devices.

The way to have more presence is literally to take your attention away from the chattering mind to focus your attention on the present moment. If you are able to stay present, you see things as they really are and are not distracted by the agitation of the mind. Not becoming identified with your mind's constant chatter also helps you to stay more connected.

Tip: To stay present with people, listen to them with genuine interest and attention. Sense their presence. Avoid paying too much attention to your chattering mind (e.g. try to stop thinking what you want to say next or whether you agree or disagree with them, and just focus on the person).

C2. Self-Awareness
"Doing one's duty, however small, in an unattached manner gives rise to the awakening of self-awareness."
—Sri Sathya Sai Baba

Self-awareness is the second and final attribute in the desire for personal mastery. Human beings are driven strongly by a sense of identity. We may identify ourselves as thinking we are "black," "white," "fat," "thin," "Christian," "Muslim," "happy," "sad," and so on. Although categorisation can be very useful for the purpose of communication, if we fall into the trap of identifying fully with these labels, we lose our awareness of self and the ability to self-express.

Once identification has been made at this level of thought, it can also lead to unbalanced emotional reactions, which we can also become identified with (for example "I am desperate," or "I am angry"). However, being aware of our emotions allows them to rise up, be expressed, and finally be released. We no longer need to spend energy fighting them if we don't identify with them, and we can release any old, buried emotions causing pain.

Tip: Meditation is the bridge to awareness. Start with focusing your attention for a few minutes every day on your breath as it comes in and goes out. Try to notice when you mind starts to wander and bring it back gently to your breath. You can choose instead to focus on your internal emotions or bodily sensations while remaining calm and observant. You should start to feel more present and less caught up in your thoughts and/or emotions within a period of a few days.

Discovery 4: Giving people what they want and what they need.

A charismatic seminar leader, whom I got to know well, had the gift of instinctively knowing what people needed. However, knowing what other people need is not enough to get people to take action and does not lead to charisma. In order to lead people, he asserted that you also need to know what they want. This is because what they want attracts their attention, and what they need gets them results.

Next time you want to communicate more charismatically, appeal to what people want as well as what they need, and watch how this transforms the message for others.

Exercises

We have defined charisma as the ability to express and be yourself fully. It follows therefore that charismatic people live a fully expressed life. The following exercises will help you to connect with what it would look like for you to live a fully expressed life. As you work through the three exercises, I encourage you to relax, take your time, and dare to dream.

Part 1: Consider for a moment now what your life would be like if you lived a life fully expressed. Imagine you're coming to the point of your passing and you look back on your life. Visualise it, hear the sounds you would hear, and feel the feelings of being in that moment.

Part 2: Then write down the answer to the following questions:

Who did you become?
What character traits will people associate with you?
With whom did you spend your time?
How did you contribute and make a difference?
What did you enjoy doing?
What did you enjoy having?

If you need some help in generating some ideas, pick a few people you admire either from history or current figures and consider what it is that you admire about them.

Part 3: Take some time out to write the story of your life based upon your answers to the questions above. Make it a great story; romanticise and idealise it to add attractiveness, and have some fun (if you wish, you can even start it with "once upon a time..."). The following are components of a great story to help you:

It must have a hero/heroine (i.e. you).
It starts in an ordinary world.
There is a call to adventure (a dream).
The hero/heroine must face challenges. The challenges must be overcome and any lessons learned described.

The challenges must be played into the hero/heroine's ultimate destiny.

Story: Living a Life Fully Expressed

I conclude this chapter with a story. It relates to a teenage girl who was becoming very agitated at home. Her parents were known to be wise, but this girl felt her father set too many rules to abide, and all she really wanted was to be free. So one day she decided she'd had enough and that she would run away—she could set up her own life by herself, free from the rules set by her parents. And that's what she did. She took her savings and ran away to the other end of the country. This girl was certainly passionate about her new life; she made new friends and was able to spend as much time with them as she wanted, wherever she wanted. Her friendships gave her a sense of meaning and she really enjoyed connecting with them deeply. She was very popular with her friends for a while, but then each friend, one by one, either moved away or lost interest, and they really weren't reliable. So the teenage girl wondered what advice her mother or father would give if she was still at home. The answer came to her in a dream: "develop a clearer sense of who you are and what you stand for." So that's what she did.

As a result the girl attracted many new friends, and she noticed that the new friends seemed to be far more reliable than the old, and they regularly asked for her opinion on things important to them. However, there was still one thing that could make her life more special: to find a great man to marry. She had dated a few young men and had tried very hard to please them, but they always seemed to lose interest. So the girl wondered what advice her mother or father would give if she was still at home, and again the answer came to her in a dream: "stay present and be genuinely interested in them as people." So that's what she did.

As a result, not only did the men she met seem more interesting, she felt totally validated and accepted by them, and in no time at all, she met a wonderful man and married him. Over time the happy couple had two beautiful children. Then one day, the children asked whether their grandparents were still alive and why they never saw them. She had always been embarrassed about the situation and nervous about what her parents' reaction would be if she ever got back in contact. She told her children she would speak to them about it in the morning and sat up late wondering what advice would best serve her children. She also wondered what advice her mother or father would give if she was still at home. Yet again the answer came to her in her dreams, and she was reminded of her father's golden rule: "courage is a habit—always take courageous action in the face of fear." So that's what she did.

She picked up the phone and called her parents that morning. She was now ready to connect with them to fully express her heartfelt love and gratitude, and at that moment she felt totally free. Her parents were delighted to hear from her and insisted on a homecoming celebration. They reassured her that they would always love her and that she was welcome home any time she chose.

How You Can Survive Chronic Illness

by Patricia Duffy

Patricia Duffy works with people who have chronic illnesses and assists them to live a life of wellness. She uses her skills as an NLP master results coach, a Reiki practitioner, and an Angel Card readings therapist, using the experience of her own personal journey from illness to wellness.

Having suffered from fibromyalgia for ten years, Patricia spent considerable time researching and learning complimentary ways in which to deal with this chronic illness. She now lives a life of wellness without the aid of any medication.

Patricia worked in a large company for many years, gaining experience in a variety of different roles and responsibilities within the organisation, including human resources, finance, and corporate business, and has qualifications in business studies and finance.

A few years ago she intensified her studies and has now trained as a Neuro-Linguistic Programming (NLP) master practitioner, Reiki practitioner and Angel Card therapist.

She has left the corporate world behind to pursue her passion, helping clients to deal with their chronic illnesses, using her experiences and her healing abilities. She has worked successfully with many people over the years with various challenges. She can be reached through her contact details below:

Website :   www.patricia-duffy.com
Email: patricia@patricia-duffy.com

My Background

I grew up on a farm in Ireland with my seven siblings, and as you can imagine, led a very active life. As with every child on a farm, I had my chores to do and regularly played in the fields and walked everywhere. From the age of ten, I was also very active in sports and continued being active when I moved to work in Dublin city.

However, in 2001 I developed neck and shoulder pains. By 2002, I was suffering aches, pains, and stiffness, and my body was frequently overcome with discomfort. I could not understand this, as I led a very healthy daily routine. I walked in and out of work, a round trip of nine miles. Additionally, on the weekends, I would walk for at least an hour and half, which I enjoyed immensely.

I even returned to my running, and still my body ached; it would ease with stretching, but the relief would not last.

In 2005, I was referred to Professor Geraldine McCarthy, the leading rheumatologist in Ireland.

My Journey

The Spiralling Road

I was given the all clear from my specialist, and my case was closed in early 2006. But in early 2007, my Fibromyalgia returned, and I had a burning sensation in my shoulders and neck. Rather than wait a year and a half for an appointment with my specialist, I sought other forms of treatment.

I researched alternative holistic treatments and therapies, and the one that attracted me most was acupuncture. At that particular time, the only available appointment was at a clinic that specialised in multidisciplinary well-being.

I embarked on a life-changing programme with food and regular acupuncture treatments. There were different stages of the programme where I eliminated certain foods, carbohydrates, proteins, etc. and introduced high-quality health products.

The benefits were amazing: I lost weight, had more vitality, and felt and looked great.

My intuition was telling me that there had to be another solution to dealing with my condition. I began to consider that the cure could come from within.

In 2007, I attended a Tony Robbins seminar in London. There I experienced a rude awakening of the power of personal evolution and how to *unleash the power within.*

As I progressed through the programme, nearing the end of 2007, I started noticing that the aches and pains were returning, so I would receive more acupuncture to relieve the pain, while continuing on the programme and taking advice from the clinicians.

By 2008, the fibromyalgia was more severe than it had ever been; I was bedridden for days, able to move only with the aid of anti-inflammatory tablets and analgesics.

The programme was too severe for me, with the result that my immune system crashed, and my chronic disease—which had long disappeared—returned.

So I was back on medication and back to regular visits to the hospital. I became allergic to certain drugs and had to inject myself every fortnight (I later requested to be taken off these medications.)

The Road to Recovery

In February of that year I received an invitation to a Christopher Howard seminar. I had been really looking forward to attending but was unable to attend because I could barely move with chronic fibromyalgia,Fibromyalgia, so I had to wait until the following October of that year.

I was so impressed by the experience that I signed up for the complete suite of personal evolution courses (Neuro-Linguistic Programming (NLP), Performance Revolution, Personal Coaching, and Hypnosis).

This was an amazing journey for me; it revealed a lot of things about myself, and I learned about anchors, limiting beliefs, and self-talk. I learned techniques that allowed me to unlock and heal my past, enabling me to cure the present and plan for a bright future. I mastered tools of the mind and became aware of the mind-body connection. I learned that in order for the body to heal, I must be congruent within myself.

During these courses, I sought out and surrounded myself with positive-minded people. These great people had encountered their own issues and experiences. We kept each other to a high, positive mindset during the courses, and we remain in contact to this day. It was during the first course that I met Caroline Dunne, who is now my great friend, advisor, coach. and my Reiki master and teacher.

Putting all these things together, I knew that this path of mindset, discovery and self-healing was the way forward. I invested in myself, and I am so proud that I did, because I am still reaping the benefits every day.

What Is Fibromyalgia?

The word "fibromyalgia" means pain ("algia") coming from the muscles ("my") and fibrous tissues ("fibro") such as tendons and ligaments. In addition to pain, most people with fibromyalgia also suffer other symptoms as explained below. Therefore, it is sometimes called fibromyalgia syndrome, or FMS. It is a chronic (persistent) condition but *does not* affect the joints and so is not arthritis.

My medical specialist explained that the muscles, tendons, and ligaments pull against each other, resulting in extreme pain and tenderness.

Some of the Symptoms Include:

Skin sensitive to touch, severe aches and pains, flu-like symptoms throughout your body
Stiffness, joint pains
Dizziness and headaches, generally as a result of neck pain
Pains around the neck and shoulder area as if one slept in a wrong position
Feelings like lactic acid buildup in the muscles and extreme tiredness, as if you had pushed yourself to the extreme
Cognitive and memory problems (sometimes referred to as "fibro fog")

Poor circulation—tingling, numbness or swelling of hands or feet

Weight Gain

Overlapping Symptoms with Other Syndromes and Diseases

Polymyalgia, which mainly appears in people over seventy.

Lupus, an autoimmune disorder, causes chronic inflammation throughout the body. It can affect any or all organs in the body.

Crohn's disease is an autoimmune disease, which affects the small intestine and can cause some joint pains and fatigue.

Irritable Bowel Syndrome, which can coexist with Crohn's and Fibromyalgia.

CFS/MME: fibromyalgia was considered part of the same illness—it was later realised that they were different.

What Causes Fibromyalgia?

With no proven cause of fibromyalgia thus far, it is a disorder that causes muscle pain and fatigue (feeling tired). People with Fibromyalgia have "tender points" on the body, points that hurt when pressure is applied. Tender points are specific to places on the neck, shoulders, back, hips, arms, and legs.

The eighteen tender points in the body that are usually highly sensitive to fibromyalgia sufferers:

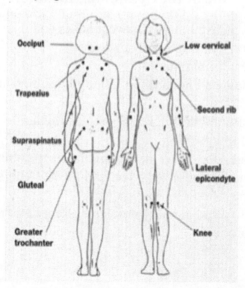

Possible Causes of the Condition:

Trauma, such as an accident, an operation, etc.
Being very active and then moving to a inactive lifestyle
Disturbed sleep at night
Depression
Injuries, general wear and tear of the spine

I have researched the subject, and it has been suggested that there are other factors that may cause fibromyalgia .However, until further research and evidence is presented to me, I contend that the above are the primary causes.

The Five Possible Conditions That May Have Caused My Fibromyalgia

Diagnosed with Crohn's disease in 1982, though it had cleared up in my intestine by 1994.

Having led an active life and then becoming inactive due to surgery in 1999.

Not being mindful of my body's injuries from when I was younger.

Car accident in 1980 where I suffered head injuries and whiplash.

General wear and tear in the cervical spine area.

My First Consultation

Professor Geraldine McCarthy, a leading rheumatologist in Ireland, diagnosed me in 2005. Before my appointment, I compiled a detailed history of my life and activities. My medical records were on file at the hospital, which she studied before my appointment as well. Within five minutes she had diagnosed me with fibromyalgia, and I was relieved that my condition had a name and that it could be treated—at that time I expected the treatment would cure it.

Is it a Common Disease?

When I was diagnosed in 2005, there was hardly any information around on the Internet or in books, or on how many sufferers existed.

People did not understand the pain I felt and how suddenly lethargic I could become at any time of the day.

About two years ago, I met five people at the company I work for, who also suffer with the syndrome. Since then I have met many more sufferers.

Today, there is greater awareness of the disease and the number of people identified has dramatically increased through correct diagnosis.

General Facts and Information

Gender: more women than men have the disease.

Age: fibromyalgia tends to develop during early and middle adulthood. However, it can also occur in children and older adults

Medical evidence reports that juvenile fibromyalgia syndrome affects 2 to 7 percent of school-age children. Similar to adult cases, the juvenile form of the disorder primarily strikes adolescent girls. Both adult and juvenile fibromyalgia patients experience widespread musculoskeletal pain, fatigue, as well as sleep and mood disturbances. Previous studies show that juvenile fibromyalgia patients are burdened with substantial physical, school, social, and emotional impairments. However, studies investing treatment for the juvenile form of the disorder are limited.

Approximately 50 percent of people with fibromyalgia have difficulty with or are unable to perform routine daily activities (Health Central, 2009)

As many as 30 to 40 percent of fibromyalgia patients have to stop working or change jobs (Health Central, 2009).

People with fibromyalgia are hospitalized about once every three years (CDC, 2009).

Disturbed sleep patterns: It's unclear whether sleeping difficulties are a cause or a result of fibromyalgia—but people with sleep disorders, such as nighttime muscle spasms, restless leg syndrome, or sleep apnea can also develop into fibromyalgia.

Family history: The genetic factor should also be considered.

You may be more likely to develop fibromyalgia if a relative has also had the condition.

Autoimmune disease: e.g. Crohn's, colitis, and rheumatoid arthritis are some of diseases from which fibromyalgia might develop.

In the middle of the nineteenth century, it was considered to be a type of rheumatism,

Subsequently it has been described at various times in many terms: fibrositis, tension, myalgia, myositis, and myosfascia syndrome to name but a few.

It was not until 1990 that it was described as a disease rather than a syndrome by the American College of Rheumatology

In 1993 the World Health Organisation finally distinguished fibromyalgia from other rheumatic disorders and accepted the definition adopted by the ACR.

Seven Things That Help Prevent the Onset of Fibromyalgia

No matter how young you are, look after your injuries; they may lead to fibromyalgia or other conditions in later life.

Don't over-exercise your body; allow the body to recover between sessions.

Everybody should start the day with a smile; a good stretch from head to toe allows the blood and energy to flow around the body freely..It is also good to move your body during the day, as most of us sit at desks.

A balanced diet with plenty of fresh fruits and vegetables.

Help move your fingers in the morning and several times a day as if you are playing the piano.

While sitting down, rotate your ankles, hips, and neck.

Reduce the amount of processed food in your diet, or eliminate it completely.

My Medical Treatment

Professor McCarthy referred me to a physiotherapist, who carried out a specific treatment called Neurostructural Integration Technique (NST)..One can only have a limited number of sessions—after each treatment, my body ached and rest was recommended. With NST, the body is only able to have about four or five sessions total, as the body has to re-balance itself and regulate itself to enable your body to integrate the treatment.

When I was diagnosed, I was put on Neurontin tablets, which I took at night to relax my body and aid my sleep. This helped greatly and relieved my body of much pain. However, as I'm not a great lover of taking prescribed drugs, I only took it when I absolutely needed it. I stopped as soon as my symptoms disappeared.

I was given aftercare instructions, which I followed for several months, until my symptoms disappeared and my life returned to normal.

How Is Fibromyalgia Diagnosed?

If you experience any of the signs above I would recommend you consult your GP, who may recommend a battery of blood tests. The only person that can diagnose fibromyalgia is a rheumatologist. Waiting times may vary from country to country; in Ireland, unless you go privately, you could wait anything up to a year.

Fibromyalgia has been misdiagnosed in the past as ME (Myalgic Encephalomyelitis).

What Triggered My Fibromyalgia?

Trauma after a series of surgeries in 1999.

Going from a very active to a sedentary lifestyle while recovering from a series of operations
Sleeping with too many pillows
Sleeping on the couch using cushions that were two hard
Ignoring sports and other injuries and continuing to train

The Four Steps of My Specialist's Diagnosis

I documented where I had pain and for how long.
I described how my pain felt on a scale of one to ten.
She checked my mobility and flexibility of movement.
She checked certain points on my body for tenderness.

The Path I Took To Be Diagnosed.

I attended a specialist regarding Crohn's disease and finally described how I was feeling, and my symptoms due of my other illness, and he referred me to Professor McCarthy.

Because I have related Crohn's issues and I'm a carrier of haemochromatosis, he had tests carried out to eliminate other possible illnesses. It was a year before I got to see the rheumatologist, as waiting lists can be a huge problem in Ireland.

"No matter how small the symptoms, one should always get checked out, as the smallest of ailment can be the biggest threat."

How Would You Know if You Suffer from it?

Fibromyalgia symptoms are similar to other syndromes or diseases that do not make it easy to diagnose. Sufferers usually have all-over body pain caused by the tendons, ligaments, and muscles not being aligned. Fatigue and tiredness descend on the body for no reason at all. Having pains in the neck and shoulder are similar to cramping and burning pain, as if you slept in a weird position that can appear at any time.

Sometimes you can have flu-like symptoms that descend on the body and disappear after a few hours.

Things to Watch out For

Neck pain
Shoulder pains, muscle knots that build up over time
Joint pains
Back pain

The Six Symptoms to Look out For

You become more sensitive to pain than normal; your skin is sensitive to touch.
Your pain threshold reduces considerably.
As time goes by, symptoms become more frequent.
Sleep disturbance: you fall asleep during the day.
You noticing twitching and spasm of the arms or legs.
You become susceptible to muscle, ligament, and tendon injuries.

What Did I Think It Was?

At first it was a mystery to me what was happening with my body, and I went down a series of routes before I could no longer stand the pain and fatigue.

I detoxed my body, eliminating certain foods and gradually brought foods back into my body over a period of time. It worked for a time, and then the cycle would start again.

I had massages, which I found to be a great relief and could last for months but then the symptoms would return. Eventually I mentioned it to my specialist, and he set up the appointment.

My Recommendation

If you are experiencing any of the symptoms above I would not advise self-diagnoses. See your GP and get him to refer you to a rheumatologist.

What Drugs and Treatments Are Available

There are several medications that may be prescribed by the medical profession to relieve the pain, which will help you to relax and assist sleep.

Anti-inflammatories and analgesics can also be prescribed to help in pain relief.

One treatment that worked for me is a form of physiotherapy called Neurostructural Integration Technique (NST).

Treatments and Therapies That
Can Relieve and Cure Fibromyalgia

NST (Neurostructural Integration Technique)
Reiki
Acupuncture
Reflexology
Certain foods—I have cut out all processed food
Exercise, daily stretching, and movement of body parts
Massage

The Five Positive Steps to Beating and
Eliminating Fibromyalgia

Find a therapy that you can do yourself—for example, Reiki, Reflexology, Meditation, Yoga, etc.

Document when you have it: record each attack in a diary and describe it in detail.

Document what irritates it, for example stress, diet, menstrual, menopause, depression.

Change your attitude to it, change your mental state and create a positive mindset, think of the words you use to describe how you feel and your condition. Use positive thoughts of how you are going to beat it.

Become aware of and understand the causes of your fibromyalgia, understanding why you have this condition is half the battle, as once you understand this, you can take positive action in your cure.

"A wise man should consider that health is the greatest of human blessings and learn how by his own thought to derive benefit from his illness." - Hippocrates

The Treatments I Underwent

When I was diagnosed, I took the drugs that were prescribed and four sessions of NST. I had to go privately for the NST, as it is not covered under the public health subscriptions.

It was a great relief not suffering aches and pains anymore; I was finally free and able to have a proper night sleep again.

My relief continued for about a year but due to an injury, my fibromyalgia gradually returned. Rather than return to the rheumatologist I looked at other cures.

How I Managed with Fibromyalgia

From where I am now, it is easy to advise you on how to manage Fibromyalgia. What I want to bring to you is how I managed before I found a cure for myself. For four years I was not aware I had fibromyalgia—my body was overwhelmed with pain, especially around my neck, shoulders, and legs. I was unable to be active in sports and could not walk to work.

In 2005, I was finally diagnosed by a specialist and began physiotherapy (NST) and medication.

How I Managed Prior to Diagnosis

I always stretched after walking including to and from work.

I took painkillers when I could no longer stand the pain.

I went for deep tissue massages.
I eliminated certain foods from my diet, such as yeast, alcohol, and dairy.

Five things That Worked for Me Short Term

1. Massages by trained personnel
2. Massaging my own body with a mixture of detoxifying oils
3. Baths with essential oils
4. Stretching
5. Swimming

How I Cured My Fibromyalgia

After several therapies and programmes, I finally came to the realisation that I would have to find a therapy that would heal or eliminate my condition completely.

Questions I Needed to Ask of Myself

Why did I suffer from fibromyalgia—why me?
What caused this for me?
What were the underlining factors that attributed to the condition?
Was there anything I could do to that would cure me?
Was I creating this to avoid doing things in my life?
Was my life in balance?
Would I have to take tablets for the rest of my life in order to live a normal life?

The Five Steps I Took to Cure My Fibromyalgia

1. I finished a journey of personal development and self-awareness.
2. I became an NLP Master Practitioner
3. I received Reiki sessions from a Sachem Master. The benefits were profound and significant.

I became a Reiki Master, which allowed me to work on myself each day

I did not want to be on drugs for the rest of my life—there had to be another way. I am now off all medication and have cured my fibromyalgia.

A huge part of my training I had to do was writing exercises around specific areas in my life. Writing about my fibromyalgia turned out to be of great benefit in my cure, and I still do writing exercises today around other issues that happen in my life.

How Can You Cure Yourself?

Let's assume that you have being diagnosed with fibromyalgia: most likely you will be given prescription drugs, which will help you sleep and relax your body at night, and also painkillers.

If you have not been referred to a physiotherapist who specializes in NST (Neuro-Structural Technique), ask your specialist.

Want to Avoid Taking Drugs?

Look at what works for you.
Find a treatment that you can afford.
Trace back when you first suffered with any of the symptoms.
Be able to cure yourself; you may have to work with a therapist.
Treat yourself to a treatment that aids your fibromyalgia once a month.

The Five Benefits of Using Natural Healing

1. Cuts down on drug taking.
2. Reduces your costs.
3. Reduces your attendance at the hospital.
4. You can work on yourself at any time.
5. You don't have to book sessions with yourself, just make the time.

Conclusion

When you are going to sleep or have a moment to meditate, ask yourself: Do you really want to cure yourself? Do you believe that you have that power?

If your answer is yes, these are steps to take if you really want a fibromyalgia-free life:

Get diagnosed by a medical expert, then take the medication prescribed.

Trace back to the first time you had the symptoms. Was there an emotional or physical trauma in the past that may have triggered it?

What caused you to have fibromyalgia? This is a good writing exercise to do, and you will have many breakthroughs and "wows." Take on board anything you feel needs attention and work with it. Afterwards it's good to burn what you have written.

You may need to make changes in your beliefs and attitudes. Love yourself first, heal yourself first, and forget about what other people are doing in their lives.

You may have to change the people around you. You are the average of the seven people you hang around with. They don't have to be drastic—make changes gradually.

Some people compound your illness; they think are serving you by jumping into the mud with you.

Others are understanding and supportive, and they will help you through it. These are the positive people who will support you in your road to recovery.

I know because I did that. I was lucky to have understanding friends around that supported me. They are positive thinking, speaking friends, and they were there to assist me overcome my fibromyalgia.

You may need to change your lifestyle. In your diet, eliminate all processed food, cook your own food, and make your own sauces. You can prepare your food in advance, freeze it, and take it with you to work, or have it when you come home.

Some people believe in vegetarian, vegan, organic, food combining and alkaline diets, as people are different in their make-up and beliefs, but here I'm sticking to the basics.

If you sleep with two or more pillows, reduce it to one. This was a recommendation made by a physiotherapist and has made a huge difference to me! It is also important to have a firm mattress and that it has good support.

Is there a therapy that you would like to study, one that you can use on yourself and does not require a huge amount of investigation, if this is not your thing? Some of the therapies are: Reiki, acupuncture, reflexology, bio-energy, yoga, and meditation to name but a few.

It is in your hands to heal your fibromyalgia, or at least keep it under control so that you do not have severe attacks, by taking small steps and then increasing them to achieve a fibromyalgia-free lifestyle; you must take control of it and not let it control you by taking the steps and actions above.

Finding a solution and a healing method cuts down on drug taking or eliminates them completely. However, I do not advise coming off medication unless it's agreed upon with your specialist.

I was lucky to have found the tools, NLP and Reiki, which helped me enormously. You can do the same—it is in your hands.

I now live a fibromyalgia-free life, and it is great, I no longer have to refuse nights or days out with friends, or rely on drugs to get me through the day.

Write your own story and finish it with a fibromyalgia-free lifestyle.

Remember: it is in your control, this is your life, and it is a fibromyalgia-free **life.**

Keys to Job Interview Mastery

by Vincent Delaney

Vincent Delaney has worked for many years in a variety of senior and middle management positions. His professional qualifications in engineering, accountancy, and project management along with years of experience have given him an in-depth understanding of people and business. During that time, he interviewed over one thousand people for a variety of both professional and skilled positions.

In the last three years, Vincent became deeply immersed in personal communications and professional coaching. He has spent considerable time and dediction being trained by some of the best personal development professionals in the world. He has now brought these strands of interview skills, personal communication, and professional coaching together into a unique product.

"My business is communication," says Vincent. "It is all about understanding how you communicate with yourself—the language that you use and the meaning that you decide to give to things. It is about how you communicate with others. It is about how you perform on a public platform or in an interview."

Vincent also believes strongly in experiential trainings, which he designs and runs. Here participants get to play full out, rather than sit and take notes. "This embeds the learnings deeply at the unconscious level," he says.

Vincent's passion is working with groups or with individuals, teaching communication for interviews, presentation skills, negotiation skills, or joint venture bids.

Business website: www.FindmeaJob.tv

Personal website: www.vincent-delaney.com

Many people are very good at what they do in their work or business. But when it comes to an interview, particularly a job interview, discomfort and self-doubt can kick in. For some it is because they feel too old, too young, or too inexperienced. For others it is the process of the interview itself they dislike.

Others go through an interview happily but don't get the outcome they desired. They think "the "right questions" did not come up, "the interviewers did not like me," or "it is all just the luck of the draw," and it had already been decided.

Some people say they would rather die than do public speaking. And for some, attending an interview with two or three interviewers is just like public speaking.

If you think you will have a job interview at some time in your future, it is time for you to take charge of the event now. In this chapter we go through four keys to a successful job interview. What do we mean by success? From the point of view of the interview, it means leaving or finishing with that feeling that you know you made a brilliant impression on the interviewers. It could be that you are made an offer there and then, or you could move to the next step of the selection process.

The most important key is mindset—but let us leave mindset until later. Why? Well, by going through some other strategies first, it will be much easier to create a focused and positive mindset throughout the preparation and the execution.

There are four keys to a successful interview. These are: Perfecting Your Story, Language, Rapport, and Mindset. Notice how these keys are all about *you*, and not about the job, the role profile, the interviewers, or the questions they might ask.

The First Key: Perfecting *Your* Story

Many people begin preparation for an interview by focusing on the job description, the role profile, and the questions they may be asked. So now let's shift it around completely. Let's start with you. What is your great story? Having worked with many, many people I have yet to meet someone who does not have a great story to tell relevant to their career or job history.

Let's break it down a little. Take some time out and recall all you have done.

Step 1: Consider separately:

Experience
Expertise
Particular achievements
Qualifications
Noteworthy events of which you are proud of what you have done

It is really important that you spend a lot of time here. If possible, involve a friend, a colleague, or a coach who will help you tease out the true extent of what you have achieved.

For example, I worked with a client who described what he did in a warehouse. He portrayed himself merely as a supervisor, but when we delved into the extent of his responsibilities, it emerged that he managed the warehouse on his own, a business that moved tens of millions of pounds sterling of stock annually, and supervised over thirty employees. The assistant manager and manager were away on some other business and rarely there. My client said that "they did not call me a manager" but had to agree he was indeed managing the operation. He was pleasantly shocked at this realisation!

Where have *you* demonstrated achievements but do not have the title or the recognition? Where are you using words to dumb-down, deflate, or negate what you do or have done? Where can you choose words and phrases that *add oomph* to your achievements? How can you tell the story better?

Another client told me of how she set up with government funding two kindergarten drop-in centres to offer help to less well-off mothers. She said that about an average of twelve children attended for a few hours per day. I asked her how long the project was running, and she said about five years. When she worked out how many children she had supported, she was astounded at what she had achieved. "About four thousand children" she said with pride. Four thousand sounds better than twelve, does it not? So, take the best six to eight of achievements. Then shrink down each instance to a word, a phrase—enough for you to remember.

Step 2: Personal Traits and Values:

Using the same process as above, identify three *traits* that really describe you. By "traits," I mean that if someone said these words or phrases back to you, you would agree that they really had you described. If it were on your tombstone (many years from now) you would agree that this was you. I must stress here that we are job focused. So examples might be: natural leader, integrity, perseverance, love the work I do, ambitious, love working with others, a true finisher. Make sure they are *your* words and not words that the job description uses.

Step 3:

Get some fifteen-by-ten-centimeter cards, which you can write on. Write one achievement/experience/trait on each card, using a large, dark coloured marker if possible. Now practice going through the cards one at a time. Take each asset and think it through. Now shuffle the cards and go through them again. The idea here is that at an interview, you cannot predict in what order you will have the opportunity to talk about a particular item.

Shuffle the cards and work through them again. Share your story with a friend or family member. Remember, this is your story. Practice it often in advance of an interview, so that you are ready to bring in your story naturally and smoothly, in any order, depending on how the interview goes. And here is another important tip: make sure that you begin each trait with "I"—the first person singular. Or at least have "I" somewhere clearly in the first sentence as you describe them. This approach is very powerful, especially for those who are very unused to interviews or those who might just get nervous.

The Second Key: Language

Language is the basis of our communication. We use language both to communicate with others and when we are communicating with ourselves.

Throughout time, words and phrases were thought to be so powerful that they had magical powers. We have Ali Baba and the Forty Thieves with "Open Sesame"—words which magically opened the mouth of a vast cave full of stolen treasure. In the legend of King Arthur, Merlin, the wizard, fought his enemies with words and spells thrown back and forth. Even St. John's Gospel in the Christian bible begins with "In the beginning was the Word, and the Word was with God, and the Word was God."

Using words and phrases can empower your communication or can do you a disservice. Simple changes in the words that you use can make your communication compelling and convincing, and can even change your own confidence and belief in yourself—that, too comes across in interviews. Even individuals who are very confident can lose out by using words and phrases that do not serve them best. The following are some of the most effective ways to use language.

1. Give the Punch Line or Headline First

Suppose you are in an interview and you are sharing a memory or story about yourself—I am assuming it is in answer to a particular question, and that what you say is relevant and that it is true. It is important that you put the punch line—*the outcome*—in first. Many people do not easily take in information until they know its relevance, i.e. *why* is it important to them. Suppose you are asked to select and describe some achievement in a previous job. First, provide the outcome or achievement. Then go through the steps or the "story" that led to that outcome. I once worked as a project manager, in an IT organisation. I reported in to the director—my boss at the time—on a fortnightly, one-to-one basis. The purpose of the meeting was to go through my projects one by one, discussing expenditure, status, risks, issues, etc. If I considered something to be worth sharing—good or bad—I would go through the sequence of events or steps that led to that outcome or issue.

I would say, for example, that we spent an extra day on gathering the information, which improved the analysis, which meant that designers finished with less effort, the build started earlier, and that we saved $5,000 on the project. He would exclaim: "*How are we ahead of budget???*" I would go through the story again, which was inefficient use of our time. He was a very focused and very capable manager, but needed a context or reason before he absorbed information. Therefore, I changed my communication to putting the punch line first. So the communication went like this: *We have saved*

$5,000 on project Win-Back. And sure enough, he would exclaim: *"How have we saved $5,000 on project Win-Back?"* And I would respond: We spent an extra day on information gathering, which improved the analysis, which meant that designers finished with less effort, the build started earlier, and that we are now $5,000 ahead of budget. So this is giving the same information but in a different order. Think of it like reading a newspaper. You get the headline to grab your attention, and now you have a context for all that follows. So give the headline first and you will hold everyone's interest.

2. Say It the Way You Want It... Not the Way You *Don't* Want It

The power of saying things in the positive cannot be overestimated. Do not tell people what you don't want, don't like, won't do, or can't do. Let me give an example of a possible conversation in an interview. I will make it a little more forceful than might be in actuality: *"I won't come in late. I won't any cause friction with my work colleagues. I won't work against the values and mission statement of the organisation. I won't let down the company when I have dealings with customers. I won't let my social life interfere with my work the following day."* What does the above make you think about? What images are you creating from these words? Ok, that might be a bit over the top, just a bit, but you can see and feel the impact of the words. If I say: don't think of a pink elephant, you think of a pink elephant. Even if you don't want to think of a pink elephant, at best it is a two-step process: first identify what you are not to think about, then think about something different. The human brain does not process negatives—at least not directly. The human brain will create images of what you have said (or written), irrespective of whether you have put a "not" or a "no" in the statement.

So, say it like you want it, not like you don't want it. Even though the brain logically accepts the "not" in the communication, the images and thoughts that are created are of the negative things. So what interviewers are remembering about you could be the negative images—unconsciously and subtly. So, if we flip the above into the positive we get: "I am very punctual—always on time, a great team player, always helpful where I can be, and I commit to working by your company's values and mission statement. I will be an exemplary member of staff, delighted to be dealing with our customers." Notice how powerful and positive this way of speaking is.

Your goal in the interview is to have the interviewers think, believe, and focus on what is to *your* advantage. So practice this yourself. Observe how you communicate with others, and notice your own thoughts and how you talk to yourself. Listen to others and how some people state the negative, i.e. what they don't want.

3. Want to, Have to, Try To

Words like "have to" and "should have" can come across implying that you have some kind of duty with reluctance or guilt that is driving you. It is far better to use words and phrases like "want to," "commit to," "will do," and "am sure to." Listen to yourself over the next few days—and to people around you. Phrases like "want to" and "commit to" show choice and dedication, rather than guilt or reluctance. This can show that you would be a dedicated and committed employee— whether or not you are being measured or monitored.

Below is a list of words that you should avoid, and across from it is the equivalent empowering word.

Disempowering Words and Phrases—don't use	Empowering Words and Phrases —use them
Try, try to	Can do
Ought to	Will do
Should, should have	Want to
Have to	Commit to
Need to	Driven to
Must do	Determined to
But, however And	
Blame	Responsibility
Fault	Accountability

As you listen to yourself and to others, you will be amazed how often these phrases are used. You will experience how the list on the right is so powerful compared to the list on the left.

4. Never Ever Use Bad Language

While the interviewers might not have a problem with strong language itself, they might disapprove *your* familiarity with them or your lack of professionalism. Don't do it! Furthermore, if there is more than one interviewer, one might be very casual with language and the others might *not*. I cannot be more direct than that.

5. No Buts, However

Be very careful using the word "But." It undoes or negates all of the sentence or paragraph before it! The best way to explain this is by way of example. Suppose I say "I am an excellent candidate for the job you have on offer. I have ten years relevant experience, I have the professional qualifications, I am a great team player, I work well under pressure, *but* I have six months experience of managing staff directly".

Ok, I have italicized the word "but" in the sentence above. Notice how it completely wipes out all the great achievements that have preceded it—it is saying that what comes after is more important than what comes before. It may be tiny, but it's a powerful and dangerous word. In most cases you can use "and" instead. If you do decide to use the word "but," just make sure you intend to negate! (Listen to people around you over the next few days using the word "but"!)

Two other words that create the same effect negative effect are "however" and "although." These sound more sophisticated and more reasonable but have the same negating result. (There, I have put a "but" in the last sentence.)

6. Brevity Leaves Impact

There is a limited amount of time in an interview, so you want to impart as much information about you as you can; you do not want to irritate the interviewers by taking too long in what you say. This sentence "brevity leaves impact" applies everywhere but especially in a job interview, or when engaging with an employer, either face-to-face or by telephone, or even by email!

When you have information to impart, or you expect to be asked about something, plan ahead and *organise* the way you will tell it.

Though don't learn it by heart—that will come across as stiff and lacking spirit.

The Third Key: Rapport

Some studies say that interviewers make their minds up about a candidate between thirty seconds and a minute into the interview, irrespective of the rest of the interview to follow. That may seem unfair—indeed it is. But that is what we must keep in mind, so build an immediate connection with your interviewers. That sense of familiarity, of liking others, is called rapport. It happens naturally, everywhere in the world irrespective of race, age, gender, or culture. Have you ever been at a party, or a social or business function, when you meet someone for the first time, and for some reason you like someone very quickly that you have never met before? You feel an immediate sense of connection and warmth. This can happen very soon after introductions.

You can observe when people have good rapport: they take on similar postures, gestures, movements, and use similar language and phrases. The truth is that *people that are like each other tend to like each other*.

It happens naturally, and when you understand how it works even at a basic level, you can achieve massive connection with others. You can use this ethically or use it to manipulate others. Let's commit to using rapport to build a positive connection between you and your interviewers that serves both you and them.

By understanding what is going on with other people's patterns of movement, language, tonality, and breathing, you can easily create a deep sense of connection and familiarity. My goal in this section here is for you to understand what is going on and use it with purposefulness.

Here are some ways to help you build and maintain rapport.

As you begin the interview, stop for an instant and imagine you are just meeting old friends. That's right, you are meeting long lost friends. Think about how you would feel and behave. This shifts the whole communication from one of possible coldness or confrontation, to one of warmth and trust. As you talk to each of the interviewers, build a sense of friendliness.

Here is the key: people that have a genuine rapport adopt the same physiology and body movement as the person they are connected with. This might seem strange or unnatural, but if you go into a bar or restaurant and observe people, you will see the unconscious "dance" that occurs. But for our purposes, all you need do is understand that there is a physiological connection between people who are in rapport.

Be conscious how quickly or slowly the other person is speaking and respond in the same manner. This really works. People who communicate slowly can get very frustrated with others who speak very fast and vice-versa. This fact alone could revolutionise communications the world over, between managers and direct reports. But when we don't know how to communicate, we think it is all just about an information dump. So if you are responding to one of the interviewers, work on tailoring how you speak to the way she speaks. It is really, really easy—in fact, we often do it unconsciously with others.

Maintain eye contact with the person you are speaking to, by way of respect and showing interest—it is not a staring competition. Note that arms folded do not mean someone is putting up a barrier or closing off to you! But for you it is best to keep your hand comfortably down. I find open palms down on one's lap is comfortable but not stiff or sloppy.

If the interviewers conduct the interview in a casual and "chatty" format, then fine: build rapport by being in the same informal mode, but do not get disarmed or lazy—that's only format, after all—this could be a major milestone of your career and you may be in competition with many other people for the job. Be positive: even if the economy is down, their company has challenges, and you have had difficulties—don't descend into the mud. If they bring up how bad things are, respond how much you relish the challenge of making a massive contribution to their company. Make them feel good! Speak from your heart and with emotion..

The Fourth Key: Mindset

Mindset is covered in other chapters of this book, so in this section we'll go through some practical ways to build and maintain your success mindset, specifically for a job interview. Already, you are steps ahead if you have been absorbing the three sections above. By understanding the power of language, and by knowing what to say and how to say it, your mindset improves. By understanding rapport it moves along further. By having your story honed and practiced, you are already way ahead. So now let us consider more ways to have that success mindset.

"If you believe you can or cannot do something, you are right."
—Henry Ford

Seven ways to build a mindset of success for your job interview:

1. Concentrate on what you want, not on what you don't want. Concentrate on successfully preparing for the interview and focus on getting that job. We spoke earlier of stating the positive in the interview. Now let us consider *thinking and living the positive*. When we keep thinking of doing badly, or of failing at something, we are unconsciously programming ourselves for that outcome. So program yourself for a positive outcome: Make a picture of a successful interview- whatever that is for you. Now think of the sounds that accompany it - maybe you or someone talking. Next think of what you are feeling, maybe elation, confidence, pride. Now turn up the brightness, the sound and the feelings. Re-create this experience regularly with as you prepare for the interview. Coaches sometimes use the negative to create expectation: "After today's session, I wouldn't expect that tonight as you sleep, your mind will be creating new possibilities. I would not expect that by the end of the week you will feel energised towards your goal." Notice that although it is said in the negative, it generates positive pictures, feelings, and emotions. The negative words merely create confusion and so add to the layering in of positive images and feelings.

2. Get used to saying the first person singular, that is, "I." Drill this into everything that you say, do, and think about. Don't wait until the interview to begin this confidence booster. When you reflect on your achievements, when you go practice your interview techniques with friends or family, coach or mentor, say: "I ran the department," "I led the team," "I sold X" amount, "I designed and built," "I achieved the best..."—work on feeling proud and good about yourself.

If you say "the team did," "we did," "the project succeeded," you get zero recognition as you cannot clearly tell what your role, responsibilities and achievements were. I have this experienced this with many job candidates and clients over the years. I have worked with many clients who found it very difficult to pinpoint their achievements. In Britain and Ireland we have traditionally been reared to be polite and never brag about ourselves, so I regularly need to trigger my clients into telling their real achievements: when I suggest they played a small part or had minor involvements in a job or a particular project, they jump to defend their true involvement.

If the job or the task under discussion involved a team, then recognise that fact. Then immediately specify the role or roles you had in the job or the project. You get no points if you don't say what *you* achieved. An interviewer might prompt you by asking "And what was your part in this?" Or they might not.

3. Be true to yourself: don't try to build a façade to hide behind at the interview. Your true self is much more impressive, and the facade is usually found out at the interview anyway. Competency-based questioning usually takes you back to past events or responsibilities. As you recall what you did, the process starts to show how truthful you are. If you are telling lies, cracks will appear in your story.

Similarly, STAR questioning probes into how you handled something in the past. You are asked about a SITUATION you were in or TASK you were assigned, the ACTIONS that you took and the RESULTS that you got.

The real you is more impressive—you will be amazed at yourself when you work on your preparation with the right techniques and the right mindset. Having coached many, many clients I have yet to meet one who did not have a great story to tell about herself/himself, and shine at any interview. Authenticity is the name of the game. Be proud, focused, confident, and authentic.

4. Check your physiology: before you commence any preparatory work, if you do not have a positive mindset, stand up, put your chest out, shoulders back, chin up, put a smile on your face, and say "Bring it on!" You need to be in the right state for the task in hand. The three components for state of mind are: *Physiology* (how you hold yourself, posture), *Focus* (what your mind is concentrating on), and *Language* (what you say to yourself, your internal dialogue). See the section above on language. This might seem a bit unnecessary, but consider this: if you are hunched forward, head down, breathing shallowly, thinking of lots of problems, and saying to yourself: "I have to prepare for this interview, which I dislike so much that I don't know where to start," how are you going to work successfully and solidly through the tasks? This is the mind-body connection. The mind tells the body about its state, and the body reinforces it by adopting the appropriate posture. As I write this chapter, I am conscious of how I am sitting and breathing. I breathe deeply into my abdomen. Every so often I deliberately make a light smile. *My body is telling my mind* what state to be in! Once you get used to this mind-body idea and know that it works, take it into the interview itself. Adopt the positive posture as

you sit down and begin. As you progress through the interview, be aware of your posture and your breathing.

5. Feedback is the breakfast of Champions.

This goes for everything in life. Sportsmen and world-class professionals both know this. Yet some people don't like to be told how improve. It goes back to when we were young. Being told how to improve is equated to being wrong or to failing. If you are discussing, practicing, or mock-interviewing with anyone, then *love* the feedback. Don't get defensive and blame the respondent. Analyse it and take it on board as appropriate. Get used to saying to people: "I know it is good, but give me three specific ways to make it better." If you have had interviews in which you were not successful, contact the company or people and seek some constructive feedback. Getting feedback is like training in a gym. At first you feel the discomfort or pain, but you progress you *seek* the pain, and even get to love the pain, because it means you are getting better and better. It is the same for job interviews—preparing for them and doing them.

6. *I want the job*. This is actually most important during the interview, but you will want to get into this mindset now as you make all the preparations. Otherwise you may not be able to switch on the "*I want the job,*" so start living it now as you prepare. And here is the deal: maybe you are not 100 percent sold on the job, or there are issues before you might accept the job, or there are other jobs on the horizon. But as you prepare, and when you attend the interview, remember: *I want the job, I want the job, I want the job.* You can turn it down afterwards, but do not programme yourself at the interview to send out signals, which *will* be picked up. Practice—I mean live it: *I WANT THE JOB.*

Some time ago, I coached an IT professional for a job interview. I drilled her on *wanting the job*. She prepared further by working with her husband like a mock-interview. After each sentence she said: "I want the job." Later while he was watching TV, she kept shouting to him "I want this job" —much to his exasperation. Yes, she was offered the job, having competed with about forty other candidates. On her feedback afterwards, the interviewers said they were very impressed by how much she wanted the job. Yes, she did truly want the job—but she *practiced telling* how much she wanted the job!

Summary

In summary, there are four keys to any job interview that you must take into account and work on. These are: mindset, your story, language, and rapport. There are all the other important considerations like understanding the job description, knowing the company, having answers to as many questions as possible, knowing about the business sector, understanding what STAR questioning is, understanding what competency-based questioning is, etc. But the four keys described above are often unknown or undervalued.

The four keys are not independent of each other. They work synergistically, which means that as one gets better, it helps the others develop too. For example, as your language improves, you feel even better about yourself and your mindset gets more focused and more positive. As your mindset gets more focused, your ability to master your compelling language improves, and so on.

And here is some more good news: These keys are not restricted to job interviews. They will assist you in personal well-being, conflict resolution, influencing others, and managing teams. Yet many, many people are not aware of them, or of their importance. Understand them, practice them—and get offered that job.

Mindset and Motivation in Property

by Gary Setterfield

Gary Setterfield is a mindset and motivation coach. He has been involved in personal development for over fifteen years. For twenty-six and a half years he worked for Nat West and Royal Bank of Scotland Group, training countrywide and at their training college for behavioural and technical skills. He has spent the last five years as a learning and development consultant, project managing the creation, delivery, and implementation of learning projects across the organisation.

In 2006 he decided to leave. His mum had died suddenly in 2001 while he was away training, and following his Dad's death, he decided it was time to reevaluate what was important. Tanya (his wife of 10 years) and he started their own multilevel marketing business and established a base of 5000 clients in two years to whom they delivered catalogues and products monthly. Continuing his education in coaching, he studied with Chris Howard, becoming a speaker, master trainer, and practitioner in NLP.

Following meeting Rob Moore, he became involved in property, and with progressive's help, he has been able to start building a property portfolio.

As a mindset coach I know how important it is in general day-to-day life to have the right attitude.

As a property investor too, I also know how mindset and motivation play a key role in your success and how you are perceived.

Property and mindset? A lot of people ask me, what has mindset got to do with property? Everything, I say, and they look at me quizzically. Mindset is the foundation to everything we do, say, feel, how we act, and interact towards and with others.

Property investing is about building relationships, ergo property and mindset are totally linked.

In this chapter I aim to provide you with an understanding of how mindset and motivation can play such a key role in your success as an investor. Of course it also goes without saying that you have to have a certain amount of knowledge too, yet it is the taking action that makes the winners stand out. As a good friend of mine Rob Moore says, "Go out and do, get perfect later."

So Let's Explore This Together.

When I mention the word mindset, what does it conjure up in your mind? Is it determination, is it focus, maybe making the correct choices, hard work, or maybe just personal development in general. You see, for me mindset is just an attitude. This was first brought home to me back in 1996 when attending a performance management training; I watched a demonstration that highlighted how powerful the mind can be when trained. One of the male delegates in our group sat on a chair at the front of the room. Around him stood four others, and all five had been asked to imagine they were either a crane for the four standing up or that he was an astronaut sitting down. They had each gone through a process to ensure they really truly believed they were that persona, and on the count of three, using only their finger tips, the four raised the chair and delegate above waist height!

This demonstration highlighted that what you believe and how passionately you believe about it can determine your performance. An attitude for me is key.

If you were to write out the alphabet letters a–z and number them as follows a = 1, b = 2, c = 3, all the way through z = 26, see how the words we may have thought of above would calculate out if you added up their respective numbers:

Focus would equal   = 64
Choice   = 43
Hard work   = 93
Mindset   = 84
Attitude however   = 100%

So how do we determine our mindset? Our mindset is determined by our state of being and behaviour, and this is determined by three key elements:

Beliefs, Language, Physiology

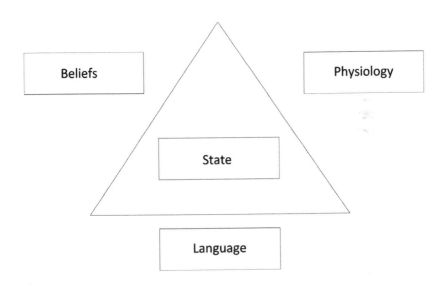

Our beliefs form the boundary of our thinking, and it's these boundaries that will determine our comfort zones and how far we think we can push ourselves. Our eyes and senses take in information from the day we are born to the day we die, at a rate of about two million bits of information every second. Now just think about that for a moment if you would: your eyes and ears are like a video camera, capturing every single image, picture, sight, and sound. If we tried to process all this information, remember it all, and make sense of it, you could probably imagine that your mind would explode, you would have total overwhelmed it. Fortunately we have a filtering system called the "Reticular Activating System" (RAS for short). Now I will not go into too much detail here, but basically it works in the same way a filter does, with its primary role to keep at the forefront information that is relevant to you at the time and to keep you safe. We have approx seven filters to achieve this task. At the same time, beliefs are also founded by your peers, parents, teachers, and your environment, and unknowingly we all have an effect on each other.

Our attitudes are also established and built upon in the same way, and what we choose to focus on similarly determines what we believe, and what we can achieve. I'll come to that in more detail later on in this chapter.

So on to language. Language is a key but not the most important element in our state of being. How we communicate with each other and also with ourselves is determined a lot by the words we use, and the tonality with which it is delivered. How we come across to others will in their eyes either inspire confidence, authority, or belief in you and your subject matter.

Words as we have said can be very powerful, and they can communicate to others a wealth of information, so what happens if you just keep telling yourself "I am great"? Do you actually feel great? You can tell yourself that everything in the world is right, that you have the best physique ever, but if it is not true, after a while the words will be empty and lose all meaning and effect.

The quickest way to affect your state of being is through your physiology, the third side on our triangle. This is probably the easiest thing to change and the quickest means of altering your state and behaviour. Let me explain: maybe you can remember those times when you have woken up feeling lethargic, tired, fed up, and generally unmotivated. Then throughout the day you walk around with the weight of the world on your shoulders, hunched slightly over, looking down at the ground as your walk. Now just as you have read those last few words, how are you feeling? Possibly a little bit deflated, sad, and generally not so great?

So let me take you now to a place, and I'm sure you remember these times, where you are walking upright, back straight, feeling tall, head up, smiling, looking around you as you walk with a spring in your step. Everything is an adventure and around every corner there is another opportunity. Now how do you feel? I'm hoping that just by visualising those two scenarios, you at some point in the first felt slouched and looked down, and then in the second you perhaps sat up a bit more, held your head up, and remembered those times when you walked with your head held high. In that short example, just by changing your physiology you also very quickly changed the way you felt.

So what have we learnt from this so far? A quick way of feeling good is by looking at your physiology. Yes, it is true today that your state can be changed by the language you use, and yes, beliefs can have an impact on your state of being, but it is equally true that changing your physiology can quickly affect how you feel, which in turn can change the language you use, and language used, if consistently positive, can then have an effect on your longer-term beliefs.

So How Does All This Relate to Property?

You may have all the knowledge in the world about property, but whether you invest using estate agents, or you speak with those selling directly (vendors), if you are slouched and looking miserable when you walk in and meet them for the first time, do you think that they will be interested in whichever words you come out with or knowledge that you have to impart? Will they have confidence in you and your abilities? If, however, you walk in smiling, standing tall, with an air of confidence about you, how much more impact and desire will they have to listen to what you have to say. From my own experiences of speaking with vendors and meeting agents for the first time, I have always aimed to walk in with that stature and posture, that air of confidence that what I have to say will be of benefit to them, and that a relationship can easily be built. With agents and vendors I always look to find out about them first; let's face it, everybody's favourite conversation is about themselves without fail.

Investing in property can provide you with the opportunity to earn from renting a passive income: in layman's terms, you obtain income for very little, if any effort. The whole idea of investing in property is that over time, history has shown that property prices will always go up. If you invest wisely and buy at the right price the value of property as it goes up equates to profit in your pocket, and as you can probably gather, this happens over time. Now, throughout the ages, we have seen property prices on average double every ten years, even when we have had black Monday, and other economic meltdowns; prices inevitably drop, but over the course of time, the value of property keeps rising.

If while the value of the property is going up, you can also make money from renting, and the rent you receive is greater than the mortgage and bills per month on that property, then you have passive income, yours for nothing...happy days!

Why would you be a property investor? You may have many reasons to become a property investor—mine is to have an income coming in each month that covers all my bills, allowing me the time to pursue hobbies, interests, coaching for the fun of it rather than to pay for my expenses. You may want to build a retirement pot for your travels, for a university bill, or maybe just to pay for regular holidays or to provide an education for your children. I know a number of investors who have built very successful property businesses, which have evolved simply because they wanted to provide their children with a university education, paid for without loans or overdrafts. They now have security and peace of mind knowing that their children will be able to study, get a good education, and not worry about the debt later into their lives.

What are your goals, why would you be a property investor, what do want to achieve? A pension, a holiday each year, debt-free Christmases, the ability to buy that special home, that beautiful car you have always wanted, taking a loved one somewhere special, buying friends gifts, paying for their holidays, being able to pay off your debts, live debt free with abundance each and every month...the list can go on. Make a list now of your short, mid, and long-term goals. Write them down where you will see them each and every day. For property investors it can get lonely because you are invariably out there alone, seeing Estate Agents, viewing properties and negotiating with either Agents, Vendors (those selling their properties) or both. It is very much a numbers game and you need to view and see a number of properties before you find the ones to suit your buying criteria, and these goals are what keep us going.

So what would you like achieve in property or just in life generally from the activities and goals you set yourself? My role as a coach is to keep you accountable for your goals and the steps that you need to take to become successful. As we have already said, being an investor can be fun: constantly meeting new people, being able to help people out from situations that bring them down, being able to support your family and provide people who are in financial hardship, enabling them to keep their homes, avoiding eviction and embarrassment.

At the same time it can be really lonely out there. It's a numbers game—just talk to anybody out there who is in property, and you will find you have to put out thousands of leaflets, sometimes in excess of twenty to thirty thousand just to get one deal, not to mention the numerous viewings, and putting in offers on loads of properties that are often unsuccessful before hitting the jackpot and the great deals. You have to have an inner determination and strength to keep on going, to overcome the objections of family and friends who do not understand the world you work in, yet are quite happy to reap the rewards with you. In climates where the economy is in despair, those not in the know are influenced by the papers saying "House prices have fallen," or "They are rising," "Interest rates are at their lowest," "Banks are not lending," etc...And there you are trying to buy houses, make money on them, borrow from lenders who will not lend, and try to show the naysayers (or "Negferrets" as I call them) that actually this is exactly the best time to be a property investor; it is also the time when you most need the correct mindset to carry you through the journey.

As we said earlier, house prices have generally gone up over time. So if they are now at their lowest then this is a great time to buy. The best time to make money on a property purchase is when you buy it. And if you can buy it at a price below current market value compared with similar properties within a half mile radius, then after you have renovated it, there is potentially the opportunity to make money, especially if you what we call in the industry "holding" the property. Keep it in a portfolio while renting it out and earning passive income.

Motivation

One of the key requirements for an investor is to be motivated. We talked above about why are you doing this, and one of the key points is once you know why, set goals to achieve the levels of income, or number of properties needed to achieve your goals.

There are two types of motivators: the "towards" and the "away from." The "away from" is the fight or flight that you may have heard about from the caveman days: when we were killing grizzly bears and fighting with dinosaurs, it was this motivation that kept us alive. Nowadays we find it more in the dieting world where we don't want to be overweight...and that motivates us to find ways of losing weight. The away from motivator is a fantastic way of kick-starting anything, from I want to get away from being in debt, I want to move away from that feeling of despair. The result is eventually we do get away from what is causing the most pain, and as a result the motivation starts to diminish, simply because we do not feel the pain any more; we have moved away from it. Then what happens? Well, we start falling back into old habits; without the drive, we may start eating more, taking less exercise, start spending a little more money on frivolous things, which although we had managed to do without for so long, have now become necessities. You can see how we can start to fall down the hill again; then the pain starts to grow again, eventually reaching the stage where it becomes too much, and so the cycle starts again.

Now the "towards" motivator is a very different animal, and it goes back to your "why"; if the motivator is strong enough, and your reason for doing it is so strong, and you have big enough goals, that will inspire you to take whatever action is necessary to move towards those goals you have set. As a mindset coach we are there to help you set goals that are stretching, that are realistic, that whatever the weather, will make you jump out of bed in the mornings because they burn so bright in your imagination. We get you to put things up on boards, to have pictures of where you want to be, and this can go down to even having phrases written on the fridge, on your computer screen, in the car, that when you see them, remind you of why you are doing this. The mind, as we have said before, can be easily fooled; it works on the basis of being unable to differentiate between fact and fiction. Studies have been undertaken with Olympic athletes where they were monitored undertaking their chosen sport. Their movements and muscles were linked to computers, and they were scanned. The results of running a race or throwing the javelin were recorded. They were then asked to just imagine in full sensory detail, to rerun that race, to rerun the throw of the javelin, and to go through in their mind, while sitting in a room, exactly what they were doing. At the same time they were fully scanned and monitored for muscle movement and brain activity. It was proven that the parts of the mind responsible for muscle reactions and body movement reacted in exactly the same way as if they had actually undertaken their sport activity.

A new way of training became available, one where there is no peer pressure, no outside influences, no arriving at the finish line after someone else, because in their mind they are trained to win.

The same with property investors: running through it in your minds won't actually get you the property or the passive income, for there has to be some effort and undertaking, yet if you knew you could not fail, what would you be, do, or have?

The same applies to walking into an Estate Agent, and we can run through the scenario with you: how would you want the conversation to go, what outcomes you would you wish to see? Then as far as the mind is concerned, the situation has already arisen; when you then go for the real meeting, the mind has already been there, done that, it's a piece of cake, sorted and solved toward the outcomes you have already planned. Now some things may not come about the way you would like them to, yet they will ultimately be more beneficial. If you can then harness that, with your physiology, which we discussed earlier, and the use of effective language, can you now begin to see what a strength and increased confidence you will have?

So how do you get started? This is a common question often asked, we have already covered the "Why are you doing it?" Linked to this is "Are you looking for capital growth or the monthly cash flow, or even a combination of them both?"

In an economy where, as we see at the moment, everything is at rock bottom, and in the words of the song "The only way is up," capital growth is unlikely to be that prevalent for a few years. That said, buy at the right price, move property on, and as we call it in the business, "flip" a property and money can be made (Flip = Buy, refurb, sell on), so possibly then cash flow could be the way forward for you. At this point it is probably important to state the following: there are many strategies out there that can be used for cash flow purposes, deal packaging, lease options, corporate lettings, HMO's (Houses of Multiple occupants) etc...People often ask me what strategy they should follow: should they go out there looking for a lease option or deal package?

I liken all the available strategies to having a tool box with different tools in it. For the budding DIY amongst you, when you go to put up a shelf, you might not be aware of what sort of wall you need to put the brackets on, stud, brick, plaster etc. If you go with the mindset that you're going to buy a property and you're taking along your tool box, then at each occasion you always will look to solve the problems of the other person and help them (the vendor directly) by building a relationship with them and knowing you have a variety of tools and strategies you can use. It is more than likely that a solution can then be found. If on the other hand, going back to our wall example, you go with a view of putting up a shelf, using only a normal raw plug in a stud wall, it will not hold for very long.

The same applies to going with just a specific strategy in mind. If you go looking for a certain deal and you have that mindset, the potential opportunities you could be missing are massive. For new investors, they are often overwhelmed by what they are or could be able to do; if you go to an agent or directly to the vendor, and you build a relationship first, get to know the person or agent, what they want, what their challenges are, what is the bottom line that they need to take away the pain. If you fully understand this, solutions can be found.

Let's now look at another potential challenge you may come across: you are new, you have found out exactly what the vendor wants, and yet you cannot solve the problem, as you are a little unsure exactly what is going to be best. This is more likely to happen where you are very new to the business, although there are always going to be new challenges arising.

This is where your power team and your mentors will come in. So what do we mean by "power team"? First and foremost these are the people that you look up to and are doing and have achieved what you are looking to achieve. In my case, my mentors have been Rob Moore and Mark Homer of Progressive Property, who between them and for their investors, have purchased more than three hundred properties. Glenn Armstrong of G & A Property. Sylvia & Juswant Rai of Berkshire Property Meet, Johnnie Cass, Master Trainer and Speaker of Unlimited Success, these are the people who have guided advised and acted as role models and mentors.

There are numerous other names that I could mention, but that would probably take up the next three to four pages. It is these people and people like them who inspire you to get up in the morning, who inspire you to achieve all that they have done. Get to know them, and talk to them; although they are big names; they are human and don't bite. Attend their meeting and courses; as Anthony Robbins says, "I stand tall because I stand on the shoulders of giants before me."

When we talk about mentors, I like to think of the characteristics below, in fact, you may even come up with your own descriptions for each of the letters—if you do, let me know. I see a mentor as having, doing, or being the following:

M   Mental strength, Masters in their field, Mind of information
E   Empower, Energy, Educating
N   Nonjugmental, Normal human being
T   Tenacious, technical, teachers
O   Obsessive, Observant
R   Resilient, Resourceful
S   Successful, Supportive

How else could you increase your education? Through reading books, listening to CD's or watching DVD's. You have already made a great start by reading this and the other insightful chapters within this book. One of the key factors with mindset is keeping focused and using your time effectively. Annotate these books, make notes, listen to the CD's in the car—your car will become your personal audio library. All these things will keep you on track towards your goals. Make time each day, particularly with books, to read and reread them, as each time you will be in a different place in your life, and you will find something different in the message. I know from personal experience that when I read a book for the second or even the third time, I always pick out things I missed from the previous time around. There is a great saying, "We don't always get what we want, but we do get what we need." This is particularly true when learning new material.

When starting out I frequently hear people say and make the mistake that they think they need to know everything before they can go and do something themself. As a result of this, very often they procrastinate and end up doing nothing. The most successful people from my experience and that of my peers are those who just get the basics and then go out and do, learning and developing as they go. It is important to remember at this point that being a property investor you are already in the top 10 percent of the population; once you have attended a course or read a book, you are already several steps ahead of others. You already will know more than most people, and it is key that you remember this, especially when attending property networking events or other property courses.

So who else can you have in your power team? You will need people who can do the things you can't or even don't want to do, because they are not your main skill. I love to use the word "Leverage" here. Leverage other people's time and skills, albeit for money, which will allow you more time to go out and do what you do best. Now the other people are brokers, solicitors, accountants, and also tradesmen to help with the refurbs. The one piece of key advice in this aspect for any of the above is find professionals who invest as well. The reason for this is that if they understand the field you are operating in, they will understand the challenges that you will face, and they will be able to provide you with the advice and support you need when you need it.

What About Challenges, Obstacles, Competition, and Rejection?

We covered this very briefly earlier. There will be occasions when any of the above will raise their ugly head. You will have challenges around, agents avoiding you, laughing in your face, sending you deals to look at that are way outside your criteria; you will be up against other investors, competition in the area if you like, and at times you will feel rejected. Remember this is a numbers game—it is part of the course of learning, so let it go! You know you can do this. I agree in reality that is easier said than done, and earlier we talked about internal language and beliefs; the important thing to remember is to keep on going. Look at it from the agent's point of view; for example, it's a Wednesday morning, and you go in to see an agent you have never seen before…you are the third person in there that morning who wants to buy houses, as last night on TV "How To Be a Property Investor" was on Channel 4, and now everybody thinks they can. From the agent's viewpoint, you are just another one, which is why your physiology, language, and behaviour are key: you have done your background research on your area, you know what you want, and you know that building a relationship is the fundamental and crucial point. Be different! Make them like you, without bribing or any brown envelopes. A very good agent friend of mine once said, "I never deal with anyone I don't like."

If I Get into This Property Investing Business What Can I Expect?

You can expect a roller coaster of a ride, and you can expect to meet fascinating people. The buzz you get from being able to help people out of desperate situations is amazing, and you'll find you have the potential to change other people's lives as well as your own, probably beyond what you can presently imagine. Getting into property for me has opened many doors that I had never even dreamed of when I was working in a corporate environment. I have met so many interesting people from such varied backgrounds, all with their own stories to tell, some with personal challenges, for example Steve Evans, who is blind, Patrick Souiljaert, who has Cerebral Palsy, not to mention those with hidden challenges, and each and every one of us has a success story within property in some way. I have so many friends that I would never have come across had I still been in the corporate world. This property business is only lonely if you try and attempt it on your own. Surround yourself with friends, mentors, networks, and forums, people you can talk too and get to know. One thing I have always found is that people are willing to share information—after all, "birds of a feather, flock together."

Taking Those Inconsequential, Little Steps

How do you climb the big hill of property investing? Property investing is no different from anything else in life—when you are just starting out, the first steps can always be the most daunting. There is no need to take major leaps, when you can take baby steps. You wouldn't run before you could walk would you? Perhaps you have seen on TV those "World's Strongest Men" competitions, where they pull trucks using a harness—initially they are on all fours, leaning forward, not noticeably moving forward, but as they lean more and more, the truck wheels start to turn, and it starts to move. Step by step they pull it further along the track, becoming easier with every step, until they are almost able to walk normally. A good couple of books you may like to read: 1) *The Slight Edge* by Jeff Olsen and 2) *The Compound Effect* by Darren Hardy. Each of these cover the same topic but from a slightly different angle, effectively, the concept expressed in the phrase "Rome wasn't built in a day," i.e. by consistently undertaking small activities and repeating them over and over again, one can attain great achievements in time.

So how does this relate to property? Take for example leafleting and post carding. You have paid for twenty thousand leaflets and have received perhaps only five phone calls, but of those five you get one good deal. You put out postcards on a weekly basis everywhere up and down the high street, each and every week, but what you don't realise is that each week you do this you are building credibility with the local community. There is the seven-time convincer rule, which says we have to see, be shown, or do something seven times before it sinks in and we act upon it. I think you get the idea. As the momentum builds, the results will follow—it all starts with taking those small incremental steps and following through consistently.

Something else to bear in mind, which I think is important in terms of how you spend your time and energy, is a principle called Pareto's principle or the 80/20 rule—no doubt many of you will have heard of it. Simply put, it is as follows:

20 percent of what you do will bring in 80 percent of your income.

80 percent of the world's wealth is earned by 20 percent of the population.

80 percent of output comes from 20 percent of input.

Think about your living room carpet: probably only 20 percent of it is actually used by foot through traffic—ok, how about in property? Consider the activities that you undertake that produce real returns or generate income. Spend the majority of your time on those few income-generating activities. Outsource what can be done by others quicker, smarter, or more efficiently. Leave yourself free to do what really matters, and that's *create* the life you really want to live.

So the only thing left to say is this:

Be excited, look out for the opportunities, and go out and do. Remember the cost of doing far outweighs the cost of not doing.

"The difference between Try and Triumph is that little Umph!"

Look forward to meeting and speaking with you whenever our paths may cross.

Afterword

And so you have come to the end of this volume of guidance and secrets to help you on your way to winning in life and work. By this stage you will have found some useful nuggets, which you are even now putting into practice. Now, I don't know whether you've noticed the positive changes these are already making to your life, or whether you will start to realise these more slowly over time; but either way, let these be a sign that you are on the right track to a much richer and more empowering life as a result of applying the many lessons you have learned from this book.

However, this is not a book to be read once and then hidden away in pristine condition, forgotten on the shelf, never to be read again.

Oh, no.

This is a book that will amply reward and repay with regular rereading.

It is a book that will bring new insights each time you read it, because you will be at a different stage in your life each time, facing different challenges and immersed in different experiences.

It is a book in which to highlight relevant sections, underline key points, and scribble inspired notes and comments profusely in every available margin! If you haven't already begun to do that, grab those highlighters and pens and get to it right away!

For in the process of so doing, you gain deeper insights and unlock deeper secrets, and that means that they will continue to serve you and help you to win in life and work.

It would be lovely to hear from you regarding some of the ways in which this book has helped you. What you have learned and discovered as a result of reading this book? What changes have you made in your life, and how have they made your life even more enjoyable?

Please do get in touch with your success stories, your comments, and your suggestions by sending an email to comments@WinningInLifeAndWork.com

Thank you, and good luck in all your endeavors and journeys through life!

Keith Blakemore-Noble

October 2012.

Acknowledgments

Conquering Shyness and Creating Self-Confidence by Keith Blakemore-Noble

I would like to thank the following people for their help in the creation of this book —all of my fellow experts who have contributed a chapter to this book, for without their contributions this would be a slim volume indeed: Graham & Urmila Phoenix, Gabi Glover, and Annette Lynch for their help, support, and encouragement throughout the project; Johnnie Cass for his help, support, and encouragement, as well as for sparking the original idea for this volume; Chris Howard for introducing me to the wonderful possibilities of a world where you can change your mind and thus change your life; and Matthew Adams for introducing me to Chris in the first place.

Living a "Not for Granted" Life by Cindi Wilson

All my life, I have been blessed with fantastic, inspirational people around me: family, friends, and colleagues. But foremost, I would like to thank my mother, Evelyn Barnes, who has always been an example of celebrating life through all the seasons and taking nothing and no one for granted. No matter what my age, she firmly reminds me, "This is the best year of your life!" I'd like to thank my sister, Sue McAdoo, who shared (and continues to share) the journey of growing up with me.

I would also like to acknowledge my very diverse, multinational friends in Luxembourg for their support and encouragement, fun, and adventure in experiencing life in foreign lands: Nicole Schaul, Cassandra Ellis, Tekla Skowronski, Helen Gresty, Diane Longdon, Teresa Pignatelli, and Marette O'Rourke and Tina Pedersen who introduced me to personal development, fire-walked with me, and continue to inspire and challenge me. I'm grateful for all the motivational speakers, inspirational authors, and personal development trainers, as well as the other participants who made me reflect, resolve, and take action! And finally, to Francis Sonnetti, a man with an enourmous heart, whose love and encouragement I could never take for granted.

Relationships Are the Foundations of Any Business by Ruth Thirtle

I would like to thank the following people: the whole team responsible for bringing this book to fruition, from my loving and supportive husband Chris who understands I work to a deadline and that can mean my working weird hours, to mentors who have helped me think differently in business, such as Chris Howard, Kerwin Rae, Duane Alley, and others (to list all of them would be another book!), Leela Cosgrove for allowing me to quote her here, and all of my friends and colleagues who have often believed in me more than I have myself.

Shift: Mindset for Success by Kim Davey

I would first like to thank Keith Blakemore-Noble for his impressive leadership and organisation in making this book a reality. To all the participants of the Academy of Wealth and Achievement, both in the UK and Australia, thank you for your incredible passion, friendship, and fabulousness! To Christopher Howard and his team of extraordinary trainers, you guys have really changed lives, thank you. To Jason, your love and friendship is unmatched. And to Annette and Stu, my incredible parents, thank you for allowing me to dream and always supporting me in everything I do. I love you guys!

Moving on from Loss: Creating the Impossible? by Ian Douglas

I want to thank my dear wife, Mimma, for all her support and encouragement, both with my writing and my ongoing personal development. I also want to thank Roy Whitten and the late K. Bradford Brown, the founders of More To Life, as well as the many fellow more-to-lifers who helped me along the way. Ditto Christopher Howard, Johnnie Cass and my co-conspirators in the writing of this book, whose ideas and feedback has been so important to me. Finally, thanks must go to my parents and grandparents, who gave me the love and challenges that provided the basis of who I am today.

Five Pillars for Supporting Women to Get Fit to Win by Claudia Crawley

Thank you to the following courageous Winning Women, who agreed to be featured and tell their winning tales: Bianca Forbes, Claire Brummell, Sarah Dunning, and Sherry Malik—I really couldn't have done it without you.

Thanks to Christopher Howard, Duane Alley, Johnnie Cass, and Annette Lynch for all that you've taught me and for the person I've become over the last two years.

Thanks also to my readers, Alison Jones and Cheryl King, for taking time out of your busy lives and for your honest feedback.

And last but not least is a huge thank you to Donal Carroll. You have a way with words like no one else and therefore raised the bar. Thanks for challenging my thinking, for your frank and constructive criticism, and for your constant support throughout.

The Secret Ingredient to Winning in Life and Work by John Brant

There are a great number of people who have assisted and supported me on my journey into leadership including many of the contributors to this book. In particular, thank you to George Metcalfe, Chris Howard, and Johnnie Cass, who have been crucial mentors and have shared with me wonderful tools for accelerated change. Without these people, I would certainly not be the person I am today. In addition, I want to thank my family for supporting me even when the road ahead looked long and bumpy, and (last but certainly not least) my wife Lisa for her assurance and patience, particularly at crucial times during this project.

How You Can Survive Fibromyalgia
by Patricia Duffy

There are many people who either assisted me in writing this chapter or were there to help in my recovery.

I would like to thank Vincent Delaney, who was there through my illness and for my recovery. If it weren't for Vincent and his passion for the English language, this book would not be finished.

The following people I want to thank. Stuart Martin, Ted Clohesey, Caroline Dunne, Eileen Daly, and Geraldine McPartland. Also Christopher Howard and his training team: Duane Alley, Johnnie Cass, Belinda Altenroxe, Paul Vernon, and Jules Cooper.

I would like to thank anyone who came into contact with me during my illness and recovery.

Keys to Job Interview Mastery
by Vincent Delaney

First, I want to thank Patricia Duffy, my partner in life, for her unwavering belief in everything that I do, and for her support in turning my passion into a successful business.

Second, I want to thank Christopher Howard and his world-class trainers Duane Alley and Johnny Cass for teaching me what I know to be the most powerful communication and success tools on the planet.

Mindset and Motivation in Property
by Gary Setterfield

A special thanks to Tanya my wonderful wife for all your help with typing and helping collate the contents of this chapter.

In addition to those specifically mentioned in the chapter, I wish to thank friends, family. and those of whom (there are many) who have supported me throughout.

Also to Chris, Johnnie, and Duane, and the Chris Howard Team, without whom none of this would have come about—thank you.

Further Reading

Conquering Shyness and Creating Self-Confidence by **Keith Blakemore-Noble**
Dale Carnegie, *How to Win Friends and Influence People* (Simon & Schuster, 1981)
Leil Lowndes, *How to Talk to Anyone* (Harper Collins, 1999)
About Me: http://about.me/KeithBlakemoreNoble
Be Your Change: http://www.be-your-change.co.uk
Ultimate Confidence System: http://www.UltimateConfidenceSystem.com
For more on conquering shyness and creating self-confidence, look for Keith's forthcoming book due in 2013.

Intimacy and Sex: The Twin Pillars of an Intimate Relationship by Graham Phoenix
Male eXperience: http://malexperience.com
How to Love a Woman: http://loveawoman.com

Living a "Not for Granted" Life by By Cindi Wilson
Barbara DeAngelis, Ph.D., *Real Moments* (Delacorte Press, 1994)
Spencer Johnson, M.D.,*The Precious Present* (Doubleday, 1981)
M.J. Ryan, *Attitudes of Gratitude: How to Give and Receive Joy Every Day of Your Life* (Conari Press, 1999)
Debbie Ford, *The Best Year of Your Life* (Hay House, 2005)
Dan Millman, *No Ordinary Moments* (H.J. Kramer Inc., 1992)
Cheryl Richardson, *The Unmistakeable Touch of Grace* (Free Press, 2005)
Meladee McCarty and Hanoch McCarty, *Acts of Kindness* (Health Communications Inc., 1994)
Leo Buscaglia, *Loving Each Other* (Ballantine Books, 1984)
Barbara Taylor Bradford, *Living Romantically Every Day* (Harper Collins Publishers, 2002)

Donna Watson, Ph.D., *101 Simple Ways to be Good to Yourself* (Energy Press, 1993)
Donna Watson, Ph.D., *101 Ways to Enjoy Life's Simple Pleasures* (Bard & Stephen, 1994)
Donna Kozik, *The Gratitude Book Project: Celebrating 365 Days of Gratitude, 2012 Edition* (Kozik Rocha Inc., 2011)
Donna Kozik, *The Gratitude Book Project: Celebrating Moms & Motherhood* (Kozik Rocha Inc., 2011)
Personal Website: http://www.cindiwilson.com
Business Website: http://www.cindiwilson.me
For more on this topic, look for her forthcoming book, *Living a "Not for Granted" Life*

Shift: Mindset for Success by Kim Davey
Napoleon Hill, *Think and Grow Rich : The 21st-Century Edition, Revised and Updated.* (High Roads Media, 2004).
Jeff Olson, *The Slight Edge: Turning simple disciplines into Massive Successes, Success Books; Revised edition* (May 4, 2011)
Anthony Robbins, *Awaken the Giant Within* (Free Press, 1992)
Robert Allen and Mark Victor Hansen, *The One Minute Millionaire*, (Harmony Books, 2002)
Paul Arden, *It's Not How Good You Are, It's How Good You Want to Be* (Phaidon Press, 2003)
Rachael Bermingham, *Savvy: Ingredients for Success,* (Hay House, 2012)
Dale Beaumont, Secrets of *Entrepreneurs Under 40 Exposed*, (Published by Smashwords, Inc. September 15, 2011)
Julia Cameron, *The Artist's Way: A spiritual Path to Higher Creativity* (Jeremy P. Tarcher/Putnam, 2002)
Vipassana Meditation: www.dhamma.org
Guided Meditations www.abraham-hickslawofattraction.com
Don Tolman:
Seven Principles of Health
www.thedontolman.com/selfcareoss/7principlesa1

Moving on from Loss: Creating the Impossible? by Ian Douglas
John Bowlby , *Attachment and Loss* (Hogarth Press/Pelican, 1969)
The Habits of Highly Effective People by Stephen R. Covey (Simon and Schuster, 1989)

Anthony Robbins, *Awaken the Giant Within* (Simon and Schuster, 1992)

Brian Tracy, *Eat That Frog* (Berrett-Koehler, 2001)

Christopher Howard *Turning Passions Into Profits* (John Wiley and Sons, 2004)

Joe Vitale, *Zero Limits* (John Wiley and Sons, 2007)

Website: www.moving-on.co.uk.

Five Pillars for Supporting Women to Get Fit to Win by Claudia Crawley

Rhonda Byrne, *The Secret* (Simon & Schuster UK Ltd, 2006)

Rhonda Byrne, The Power (Simon & Schuster UK Ltd, 2010)

Brian Tracy, *Goals!* (Berrett-Koehler Publishers Inc 2004)

Karen Kimsey-House, Henry Kimsey-House, Laura Whitworth, and Philip Sandhal, *Co-Active Coaching* (Davies-Black Publishing 2007)

Julia Hastings, *You're Great* (Touchstone Publications Ltd 1997)

Julia Hastings, *You Can Have What You Want* (Touchstone Publications Ltd, 1997)

Stephen R. Covey, *The 7 Habits of Highly Effective People* (Simon & Schuster UK Ltd, 1999)

Napoleon Hill, *Think and Grow Rich* (Vermilion, 2004)

Website: www.winningpathwayscoaching.com

The Secret Ingredient to Winning in Life and Work by John Brant

Robert B. Cialdini, *Influence: The Psychology of Persuasion*

Rick Frishman and Jill Lublin, *Networking Magic*

Shelle Rose Charvet, *Words That Change Minds*

Shelle Rose Charvet, *The Psychology of Persuasion*

How You Can Survive Fibromyalgia by Patricia Duffy

Louise Hay, *You Can Heal Your Life*

Louise Hay, *Heal your body A–Z*

Marie Lawson Fiala, *Letters from a Distant Shore*

Dr. Wayne Dyer, Change Your Thoughts, Change Your Life

If you are not a big reader you can get some of these on audio.

Keys to Job Interview Mastery by Vincent Delaney
Jack Canfield, *The Success Principles* (Free Press)
Robert B. Cialdini, *Influence: The Psychology of Persuasion* (Collins Business)
Stephen R Covey, *The 7 Habits of Highly Effective People* (Free Press)
Malcolm Gladwell, *Outliers: The Story of Success* (Little, Brown & Co.)
Business website: www.FindmeaJob.tv
Personal website: www.vincent-delaney.com

Mindset and Motivation in Property by Gary Setterfield
Michael Heppel, *How to Be Brilliant* (Pearson Education Limited, 2004)
Jeff Olsen, *The Slight Edge* (Success Books an imprint of Success Media, approx 2005)
Darren Hardy, *The Compound Effect* (Success Books an imprint of Success Media, approx 2010)
Rob Moore and Mark Homer, *The 44 Most Closely Guarded Secrets* (Trafford, 2007)
Rob Moore and Mark Homer, *Make Cash in a Property Market Crash* (Progressive Property Limited, 2008)

Contacts

Conquering Shyness and Creating Self-Confidence: Keith Blakemore-Noble
> About Me: about.me/KeithBlakemoreNoble
> Be Your Change: www.be-your-change.co.uk
> Ultimate Confidence System: www.UtimateConfidenceSystem.com
> Personal website: www.Blakemore-Noble.net

Intimacy and Sex: The Twin Pillars of an Intimate Relationship: Graham Phoenix
> Male eXperience: malexperience.com
> How To Love A Woman: loveawoman.com

Living a "Not for Granted" Life: Cindi Wilson
> Personal Website: www.cindiwilson.com
> Business Website: www.cindiwilson.me
> LinkedIn: www.linkedin.com/in/cindiwilson

Relationships Are the Foundations of any Business Ruth Thirtle
> Your Abundance Now: www.abundantyou.com/

Shift: Mindset for Success: Kim Davey
> Personal website: www.kimdavey.tv
> Business Website: www.nzdancenetwork.co.nz

Moving on from Loss: Creating the Impossible? Ian Douglas
> Website: www.moving-on.co.uk.

Five Pillars for Supporting Women to Get Fit to Win: Claudia Crawley
> Website: www.winningpathwayscoaching.com

The Secret Ingredient to Winning in Life and Work: John Brant
LinkedIn: http://www.linkedin.com/pub/john-brant/19/676/934

How You Can Survive Fibromyalgia: Patricia Duffy
Website: www.patricia-duffy.com
Email: patricia@patricia-duffy.com

Keys to Job Interview Mastery: Vincent Delaney
Business website: www.FindmeaJob.tv
Personal website: www.vincent-delaney.com

Mindset and Motivation in Property: Gary Setterfield
Website: www.garysetterfield.com
Email: info@gtpartnership.com
home@gary.setterfield.name

Printed in Great Britain
by Amazon.co.uk, Ltd.,
Marston Gate.